THE LEGAL SEA FOODS COOKBOOK

THE
Legal Sea Foods
COOKBOOK

George Berkowitz
and Jane Doerfer

Illustrations by Bruce Hutchinson

Doubleday
NEW YORK
1988

Library of Congress Cataloging-in-Publication Data

Berkowitz, George.
  The Legal Sea Foods cookbook.
  Includes index.

  1. Cookery (Fish) 2. Cookery (Seafood) 3. Legal
Sea Foods (Restaurant)   I. Doerfer, Jane.   II. Legal
Sea Foods (Restaurant)   III. Title.
TX747.B39   1988   641.509744'61   87-8922

ISBN 0-385-23183-0 (pbk)
ISBN 0-385-19830-2 (hc)
Copyright © 1988 by George Berkowitz and the Jane Doerfer Literary Trust. Harriet
Berkowitz. Roger Berkowitz. Marc Berkowitz and Richard Berkowitz

Acknowledgments

I could not run Legal Sea Foods without my family: my wife, Harriet, and our sons, Roger, Marc, and Richard. Harriet suggested opening a restaurant and worked alongside me to get it established. Roger and Marc, who gave us a hand peeling shrimp and sweeping floors when they were twelve and ten, have developed into two of the most competent and creative restaurateurs in the country. Although our youngest son, Richard, is still in college, he has worked as a waiter, expediter, and fish handler. Should Richard choose to enter the business I know he'll prove to be as successful as his brothers.

Jane Doerfer, my co-author, not only helped me write the text but also developed recipes that tasted delicious and were easy to prepare. That's always been our philosophy at Legal Sea Foods, and Jane understood it well.

I am grateful to Vicki Kelley, who is an associate professor at Harvard Medical School, for reading the chapter on why fish is good for you and offering her comments.

Our editors at Doubleday, Lindy Hess and Harold Kuebler,

have been enthusiastic about the book from the beginning and have shepherded it along the way. Larry Moulter came up with the idea of the book, Alex Godfryd at Doubleday supervised the art work, and Randall Mize was the designer.

We were so impressed with Bruce Hutchinson's artistic ability that we hired him to illustrate our menus. When we needed an illustrator for this book, Bruce was a natural choice. Bruce is a talented young man whose illustrations evoke the essence of the sea.

Finally, I would like to dedicate this book to my father, who taught me that top-quality merchandise and good business go hand in hand.

Contents

The Legal Sea Foods Tradition   1
Why Fish Is Good for You   9
Selecting Fish   15
Catch of the Sea   21
Basic Techniques for Cooking Fish   37
Our Favorite Fish Recipes   55
Shellfish   103
Shellfish Recipes   127
A Mélange of Soups, Salads, and Basic Recipes   155

INDEX   175

NOTE: Whenever the name of a recipe is capitalized, the recipe is included elsewhere in the book; see the Index for page numbers.

THE LEGAL SEA FOODS COOKBOOK

The Legal Sea Foods Tradition

Twenty years ago, when Harriet and I opened our first restaurant in Cambridge, Massachusetts, we had three employees: Harriet, myself, and a man who fried fish. Now, we have six restaurants throughout the state and a payroll of more than a thousand. Every day we serve about eight thousand customers. Harriet and I no longer work in the restaurants, but our sons, Roger, Marc, and Richard, are on hand to ensure that our Legal tradition for quality continues.

My father began the family's reputation for providing quality foods in the early 1900s when he started the Legal Cash Market, a meat market and grocery store on Inman Square in Cambridge. He named the shop after the Legal trading stamps that he passed out with the groceries. (These stamps were the forerunners of S&H green stamps.)

He stocked only the best grades of meat, such as prime beef, in an era when most butchers were satisfied with lesser grades, such as choice. Along with my brothers, I worked at the market, and eventually my father let me do some of the purchasing. Every day he would send me down to the wholesale dealers to pick out the meat. If I selected a pork loin that was too fatty or didn't look right, my father would dispatch me right back to the market to try again. I quickly learned that the only way to satisfy him was to buy top-quality meat.

One of my cousins, who was the head meat buyer for a chain store, suggested that the area could use a really good fish market. I couldn't tell a haddock from a cod, but in the early 1950s I decided to take over a store located next to my father's. I called my store Legal Sea Foods to point up the connection with my father's shop.

Very early in the game I found out that there are no bargains in the fish business. Anytime fish is offered cheaper than it should be, it usually means that the wholesaler is getting ready to dump it.

Top-quality fish always commands top prices. One day I succumbed to one of the bargains—haddock at a cheap price. All week long I lay sleepless worrying about whether I had sold my customers poor-quality fish. I had worked so hard building up the business only to risk losing my best customers merely to save a few cents. From that moment on I vowed that I would never again sell fish that was less than 100 percent.

Our reputation as a good place to buy fresh fish snowballed when the Japanese community at Harvard and MIT started touting the store as the best place in Boston to buy raw fish for sashimi. Pretty soon people came from miles around to buy fish at Legal, and our business was established. (Eventually, we even opened a Japanese and Chinese grocery store for these customers. I made special trips to Chinatown to buy fresh tofu and bean sprouts to stock at the shop.)

By the mid-1960s, we had moved our fish market into a section of my father's store, and when he retired, we had an opportunity to expand into the whole building. When Harriet suggested opening a restaurant, I thought she was crazy, because we were overworked as it was. We knew nothing about the restaurant business—we only knew good fish. In a way, though, that was an advantage, because we didn't have any bad habits to unlearn.

We hired a carpenter and started remodeling, working nights and part time, converting the meat-market area into a restaurant. Believe me, this was a low-budget operation—in 1967, the conversion cost us about $2,400. Our kitchen consisted of four or five Frialators, a broiler, and the commercial walk-in refrigerator my father had used to store meat.

The restaurant was set up with long tables and benches at which people ate family style. (It was cheaper that way.) We provided plastic utensils that could be thrown away because we didn't even have room for a dishwasher. We didn't advertise. We had no money to advertise. We just opened the doors and started serving food.

From the beginning, Legal Sea Foods was a family business. Harriet worked with me behind the counter, and ran the cash register. Our sons Roger and Marc, who were teenagers, arrived after school to peel shrimp, sweep floors, and do other menial tasks. When they grew tall enough they worked behind the counter, serving customers. Harriet's father, Max, also ran the cash register, and got paid off in fish. For a while Harriet's mother, Annie, helped out wrapping plastic dinnerware in paper napkins.

I soon discovered that running a restaurant was a little different from operating a fish market. In the restaurant business there are no days off—I was working seven days a week. My day started at 6 A.M., when I picked up the fish at the wholesale fish markets on Atlantic Avenue in Boston where today the waterfront park is located. I bought from different dealers. Some had flatfish, while others handled Italian specialities such as squid, sardines, and octopus. When the day fishing boats arrived, I purchased fish directly off the boats. I spent the early-morning hours going from dealer to dealer picking out the best catches of the day.

By 8:30 A.M. I was back at the restaurant. I set up the fish-market case and started cutting the fish into the portions to be served at lunchtime—which was a pretty simple process, because we served fish only two ways—fried and broiled. (At times I ended up not only cutting the fish but also cooking it, because there were always cooks who didn't show up.)

We opened the doors at 11:30 A.M. for lunch. In those days haddock, our customers' favorite selection, was about fifteen cents a pound wholesale, so we could keep the prices low. Once the lunch crowd abated, we started all over again preparing for the dinner rush. At 9 P.M., when the restaurant closed, we had to clean up and get set for the next day's onslaught of customers. Many weeks I averaged one hundred working hours.

I don't recall this time with great nostalgia, nor would I like to repeat the experience. The weeks sped by in a blur of fatigue, when it seemed all I did was work and sleep. Harriet was my solace. I was working with my hands and it seemed I would be stuck doing that forever. She encouraged me to think about the future, and worked alongside me to improve the business. For novices, we were lucky. We didn't make too many mistakes, and the ones we made weren't big enough to put us out of business.

Our big break came about six months after we opened, when Anthony Spinazzola, the restaurant critic of the Boston *Globe*, reviewed our restaurant. The review came out on a Friday morning. It was a great review. (He complained only about some papers on the floor.) That evening the line of customers was right out the door and down the street. We ran out of fish. From that day on there has always been a line at Legal Sea Foods.

Harriet and I decided that we would treat customers the way we wanted to be treated when we went out to eat. We served each customer the moment his order was done rather than waiting until the order was ready for the entire table. This procedure guaranteed the freshest-tasting fish.

As I was always in a hurry, I disliked waiting to receive the bill at the end of a meal. That's the real reason why for many years people paid their bill the moment they placed an order at Legal Sea Foods. I also objected to paying extra for coffee, so until recently coffee was free at our restaurants. To this day, waiters and waitresses serve whichever customer needs assistance, and pool their tips, so that service is as efficient as possible.

People hate to eat alone. If you go into many restaurants by yourself, the hostesses make you feel worse by seating you last. We had a rule that if a single person walked in, he would be seated first so he wouldn't have to stand around waiting.

The backbone of our menu has always been fresh fish cooked simply. We didn't run a gourmet restaurant where the chefs had the luxury of spending as much time as they wanted preparing a sauce from scratch. We had to feed people quickly in order to keep the volume of customers high and the prices low. Saving time was of utmost importance. I figured out the quickest way to fry and grill fish and perfected a method for broiling fish that Julia Child wrote up years ago in her book *From Julia Child's Kitchen.* (You don't turn the fish—for more information read the chapter on cooking techniques.)

Julia knew our operation firsthand. When she and her husband, Paul, moved back to Cambridge, she asked her hairdresser to recommend the best place to buy fish. The hairdresser suggested us, and Julia has been buying her fish at Legal ever since.

In the early 1960s, when Julia began taping the French Chef programs for WGBH-T.V. in Boston, I supplied the fish for the series. One show I'll never forget was the program she did on swordfish. I got Julia a two-hundred-pound swordfish, and lugged it over to the studio. At the time I couldn't afford to lose it, so I stood by to keep the swordfish iced down right up to the moment she shot the scene, and then rushed it back to the market to sell.

When Julia cut into the swordfish she used a magnificent French serrated knife that was at least 2½ feet long. I remarked what a wonderful knife it was, and Julia told me that the next time she went to France, she'd bring me back a similar knife.

Sure enough, six months later Julia walked into my store with a gift-wrapped package inscribed "Bon Appetit, Love Julia." When I opened the package, I found a duplicate of the knife she had used on the program.

I still have the knife.

Now that we're well established, people often ask what my long-range plans were when we started—as if there were a formula they could copy to ensure success. I would have to say it was a combination of hard work and quality food at reasonable prices. I wish I could claim that the rapid growth of Legal Sea Foods was part of a grand design I plotted in advance, but twenty years ago all I wanted to do was to pay my bills and to provide a good living for my family. Frankly, if it weren't for our sons, I might still be running that small restaurant in Inman Square in Cambridge. Because Roger and Marc decided they wanted to work in the business, I was able to expand the number of restaurants we ran and still have a family member on hand to oversee the day-to-day operations of each restaurant.

Family businesses are rewarding, but they have their own inherent weaknesses. When I was part of a special program for entrepreneurs at the Harvard Business School, we studied case histories of family businesses that had problems. We learned that operating a successful family business requires special skills. It's not enough to be an entrepreneur and to have a good product, because if the family members can't work together in harmony, the family falls apart—and the business seldom thrives. Too often the founder is unaware (or chooses to overlook) how easily rivalries and jealousies can develop among siblings.

I was aware of the potential for problems before I went back to school at Harvard, but that experience allowed me rethink the way we operated and gave me an orientation from a philosophical as well as a practical view of how a viable family business should exist. Our sons, Roger, Marc, and Richard, are bright and aggressive, and possess the entrepreneurial spirit in abundance. I'm a parent as well as a businessman and want my sons to feel free to carve out their own niches in the organization. I run the company. Roger and Marc operate some of the busiest restaurants per square foot in the country. I've almost taken for granted their ability to do this competently. I know only too well how difficult it is to handle a huge volume of business and to keep the quality of food high. Roger runs the restaurants in Boston, Cambridge, and the northwestern suburbs. Marc manages the restaurants in Chestnut Hill and Worcester and the Logan Airport lobster concession.

I am very proud of their achievements and the fact that neither has been satisfied to sit back and live with the status quo. Roger is particularly interested in wine. Within a few years, under his direction, Legal has developed one of the best wine selections of any restaurant in the country. He initiated a computer printout of our wine choices, which describes each wine in detail and allows us to continually update our inventory.

Marc saw the potential in the take-out gourmet food area, and has opened a facility in Chestnut Hill that I consider one of the best on the East Coast.

Richard, our youngest son, is only twenty-two and still in college, but he's already worked in several divisions of the company and has an excellent grasp of the fundamentals of the business. Like his brothers, he is a workaholic, and I foresee a great future for him as part of the Legal Sea Foods operation.

I hold staff meetings once a week to discuss current problems, new products coming into the restaurants, and our plans for future growth. When I listen to my sons and the other capable management people who have recently joined the company, I often ponder how wonderful it is when young people have great ideas and expectations. There's almost no limit as to where they want to go. Their vitality is contagious.

In the future, we will be adding a few more restaurants in the Boston area and expanding westward. This kind of growth wouldn't be possible without my hard-working family and the qualified young men and women on our staff who want to grow with us and understand the Legal tradition of quality foods set down by my father so many years ago.

Why Fish Is Good for You

You might expect that as the owner of a fish business I have been happily eating fish all my life. Actually, I never ate fish at all until I was about twenty-five years old. When I was growing up (and money was tight) we consumed whatever meat was left unsold at my father's meat market at the end of each day. My mother didn't care for fish; like other people, she worried that we would choke on the bones.

I had no interest in fish until we opened Legal Sea Foods. Then I decided that since I was selling fish, I ought to know how the different varieties tasted so that I could answer our customers' questions intelligently. At first I favored blander fish such as haddock and cod, but after a while I began to crave fish with a stronger flavor, like mackerel and bluefish. By sampling different kinds of fish—and cooking them every which way—I discovered that fish are an amazingly versatile food; just a switch in cooking techniques from frying to baking makes even a single variety taste different. Now I eat fish at least once a day and can't imagine going back to a meat-based diet.

Harriet and I care about what we eat. For many years we've favored a diet that's high in fish, fresh fruits, and vegetables, and low in fats and carbohydrates. I was not the least bit surprised when medical studies heralded the findings that a fish diet is much, much healthier than one consisting almost entirely of meat. I already knew that when I ate fish I felt better than when I ate meat. In fact, my desire for meat has just about disappeared, although I'll occasionally hanker for a steak or lamb chop. After all this time eating fish, I find meat hard to digest and far too fatty for my taste.

Fish is much easier to digest than meat because it contains a smaller amount of connective tissue and short, rather than long, fibers. The connective tissue in fish breaks down at a relatively low temperature becoming flaky and easily digested. In addition, fish includes little fat. For example, haddock has less than 1 percent fat while pork has about 21 percent (and cheese a whopping 32 percent). The fat in fish is mainly polyunsaturated and monounsaturated. (Saturated fats, such as those found in meat, cause the cholesterol level in blood to rise.)

In addition, fish is high in protein. At Legal Sea Foods, our portions of fish range from 8 ounces at lunch to 12 ounces at dinner. Yet even a small 3½-ounce helping of a white-fleshed fish contains about one third of an adult's recommended dietary allowance for protein, with the bonus of almost no fat, and fewer than 100 calories.

Scientists around the world have been working on ways to prevent heart disease. Recent studies have shown that certain fish—particularly fatty fish—contain a fatty acid known as omega-3 that actually helps prevent the formation of clots in the blood (a cause of heart attacks) and to a lesser degree lowers cholesterol levels in the blood.

Researchers are also now working on clinical trials to establish the link between eating fish oils and the body's ability to resist diseases such as lupis and kidney disease. Studies are also going on to ascertain whether a fish-based diet will lessen the chances of breast cancer in women.

The evidence is overwhelming. Fish not only tastes good, and is an excellent source of protein, but also can help prevent some of today's most serious diseases.

Of living creatures, fish, and only fish, contain omega-3. (Leafy green vegetables and soybean oil are other sources.) Why are fish and shellfish the main source of omega-3? Omega-3 comes from the plankton in the ocean the fish eat. The fish larvae eat plankton, the small fish and shellfish eat the larvae, and they are in turn are consumed by larger fish—and as this food chain continues, omega-3 becomes concentrated in the oils of the fish. North Atlantic waters are teeming with plankton—that's what gives our ocean its characteristic green hue, and what makes our fish more healthful as well.

All fish are good for you, but the fish that contain the greatest concentration of omega-3 are the fatty fish, such as mackerel, bluefish, salmon, sardines, eels, bluefin tuna—and rainbow trout. I often snack on sardines because I like their taste, but they are also one of the most healthful foods I could consume. Sardines contain large amounts of omega-3, as well as a high percentage of minerals such as calcium because they are packed with the bones still in the fish. Shrimp, clams, and oysters have more calcium than most fish, and are much higher in calcium than meat. Oysters are loaded with zinc.

Until recently, we all assumed that fish would continue indefinitely as a plentiful and inexpensive protein source, but overfishing and pollution have endangered many species of fish. When foreign fishing fleets, such as those of the Russians and Japanese, overfished the Georges Bank area off the New England coast, haddock almost disappeared from North Atlantic waters. (The Russians ruined fishing in the Baltic Sea after World War II when they used it as a dumping ground for chemicals.) These activities gave impetus to the government's establishing the two-hundred-mile limit and closing the fishing grounds during haddocks' spawning season (called "putting up the fence"). These conservation measures seem to be working, although haddock remains in short supply.

Commercial fishing in polluted rivers, such as the Hudson River in New York, has been prohibited. Safeguards like these, and increasing public awareness, lessen the chances that you will eat fish contaminated with industrial compounds such as PCBs, that are retained in the fat of fish. I sit on the board of the New England Fisheries Development Foundation, a nonprofit trade association of fishermen, processors, and marketers of seafood, and I am a director of the Massachusetts Marine Fisheries Advisory Commission. I've watched firsthand the way people in the industry and government are working together to preserve this finite resource. In this country we were late in implementing safeguards to protect our fish, but we're making up for lost time.

Europeans have the reputation of guarding their natural resources carefully. Yet, I've seen packaging practices in Europe that would be shunned in the United States. In the Shetland Islands off Scotland I watched haddock no more than five inches long being filleted. In Denmark I saw fishmongers sell flounder fillets that weighed no more than one ounce. The Danes have a shortage of flounder; much of the flounder they sell is trucked in from Holland. Unless they start conserving their fish resources, as we are attempting to do, fish will become a rare treat for many Europeans.

I would hope that increased public awareness and greater conservation measures on the part of government and fishermen alike would guarantee that around the world people would continue to have a supply of one of the finest-tasting as well as one of the most healthful foods there is to eat.

Selecting Fish

Fish must be fresh to taste good. This statement sounds obvious, but you'd be surprised how many people ignore it. They buy fish for dinner, then decide to eat out. Two days later when they finally cook it, they grumble that the fish has a mushy texture and mediocre flavor. These cooks have forgotten the first rule of cooking fish: buy fresh fish and cook it the same day. Storing fish loosely wrapped in the refrigerator can stave off spoilage only for a short while.

It's important that you realize how fish is treated before you buy it at the market because there's no government grading of fish as there is for meat. Meat has to measure up to certain specific standards, but the only standard for fish is whether or not it is fresh.

In turn, the freshness of fish completely depends upon how skillfully it is handled and how far along its aging process it has progressed. There are many steps from the moment a fish is caught and the time you buy it at the market. Any weak link along the line rapidly diminishes the quality of the fish.

When I first opened Legal Sea Foods, customers would occasionally come back and claim the fish they had bought was tough. I found that hard to believe until I discovered that fish have to age slightly—just like meat. When a fish dies, its muscles tighten up and it goes into rigor mortis (which I prefer to call rigor). Commercial fishermen, by putting their catch on ice as soon as possible, use rigor to their advantage, because the longer a fish remains in rigor, the better it keeps. (Rigor is essentially a holding action.) Some large fish stay in rigor between two and four days, while small fish come out of rigor quickly, often in a matter of hours.

(Many sports fishermen would deny the existence of rigor because they don't ice down their fish immediately after they are caught. Instead, the fishermen either allow the fish to stay in the heat of the sun, which prematurely ages them, or they troll the fish on lines behind their boats, which also ages them because the water is too warm.)

Once a fish comes out of rigor, its muscles relax again, and it is ready to cook. At this point the fish is at its optimum point of flavor, but at the same time it is also highly perishable. Unlike meat, fish have cold-tolerant bacteria that can continue growing even under refrigerated conditions. An exception to this is tropical fish, which do not have these cold-tolerant bacteria, and therefore will keep longer under refrigeration.

How can you tell whether a fish is fresh or on the verge of spoiling? A fresh fish looks bright; the skin is bright and moist; the eyes are clear and bright; and the gills are a bright red. As the fish ages the flesh dulls and dehydrates, the eyes turn cloudy, and the gills turn a brownish color. The cavity of a fresh fish smells fine; only a fish on the verge of spoiling has an off odor. When you press down on the flesh of a fresh fish, it springs back. When the indentations from your fingers remain, the fish is not fresh and you should not buy it.

The same principles apply for filleted fish. Keep in mind that a fish is composed of about 70 percent water. As a fish fillet is exposed to the air it loses moisture, becomes dehydrated, and its flesh flakes more easily. A fresh fish fillet is firm-textured. When you buy an uncooked fish fillet that practically falls apart in your hand, you have bought "old" fish.

You can make your life easier if you take the time to locate a good fishmonger who prides himself on the quality of his fish. If I were new to an area, I would ask for recommendations from people who like to cook.

Don't count out the large supermarket chains, either, because many supermarkets are trying to upgrade the quality of their fish. You should be aware, however, that several large chain stores now sell fish that have been dipped in a salt brine to give them an extended shelf life. The fish keep longer, it's true, but they also have a salty, artificial taste that is unpleasant. At Legal Sea Foods, we don't buy fish that has been brined—nor should you. If you ask him, the store's fish buyer generally will explain how he handles the fish he sells. If he sounds evasive, examine the fish's surface; an almost artificially shiny appearance is one tipoff to brined fish. Also, if you run your hand along the skin, and it feels slippery, the fish may have been brined.

When you get home, immediately refrigerate the fish in the coldest part of the refrigerator near the back (or in the meat compartment), loosely wrapped in waxed paper until you are ready to cook it. If your refrigerator tends to dry out food, cover the fish with moistened paper towels.

We guarantee the quality of fish at Legal Sea Foods by buying fish daily, and only buying the best. Every weekday morning between 5:30 and 6 A.M. our fish buyer can be found at the fish auction held in a crowded room in one of the buildings at the Fish Pier on the Boston waterfront. Other wholesale fish buyers vie for the fish, but they know that we pay top dollar to get what we want.

The kinds of fish being offered are posted on a huge blackboard. The auctioneer sells the fish in about thousand-pound lots straight from the boats. Sometimes, you'll hear an offering for "over the road" fish that is trucked down from Canada. These fish will sell for less than the freshly caught fish.

Large fish for sale, such as cod, already have been butchered and gutted on board the commercial fishing boats. The fish arrive packed in ice, bellies down so that water doesn't collect inside their bodies. This process gives the fish a longer shelf life because there is less bacteria in the fish to cause spoilage. Small flat fish, such as flounder, are left whole.

As you might expect, the most popular fish, such as haddock, command the top prices while species such as pollock and cusk sell for a fraction of those amounts. There's nothing wrong with these fish—they're just not as well known, although they are in good supply.

Once the auction is over, our buyer shops at the wholesale fish houses on the waterfront for items such as shrimp or squid not sold at the auction. His early-morning buying completed, our buyer packs our refrigerated truck with thousands of pounds of fish.

My staff knows that I am a zealot for cleanliness. From the moment the fish is loaded into our sanitized barrels, and placed in our refrigerated trucks, it is exposed only to optimum conditions. All the fish is processed at our commissary, where we can control these conditions to my satisfaction. (We keep the temperature of the fish-cutting room and the production area at 45 degrees F. so the food won't deteriorate.) I've recently set up a laboratory so we can spot check the quality of the shellfish we sell. All our shellfish comes from government-certified areas, but I like to be extra careful.

We process more than one hundred thousand pounds of fish a week at the commissary, just about all of which is consumed in the restaurants. Our crew of fish cutters custom-cuts all the fish by hand rather than trimming it by machine. This way we end up with better pieces of fish that don't break up during cooking. We are one of the few fish restaurants in the United States that still takes this step.

By midmorning the fish have been cut up and sent out to our restaurants and fish markets, where they continue to be refrigerated or kept on ice until the time they are either cooked or sold. During the midafternoon we send another shipment of fish so that the supply is replenished. The entire fish-cutting and production areas are sanitized continuously, and receive a thorough going-over at the end of each day.

You might consider these precautions a lot of unnecessary fuss for fish that will be sold the same day we buy them, but I have always believed that it's both common sense and good business to protect the quality of the fish we handle.

I can taste the difference in the fish we sell, and so can our customers.

Catch of the Sea

Let's assume that you are standing at the counter of the best fish market in town. The fish looks terrific. It's fresh, and the selection is excellent. You're toying with the idea of making a fish stew for dinner. Both the haddock and cusk look good. The cusk has the advantage of costing far less than the haddock—but you don't know much about it. Finally you decide to buy the haddock, and vow to try the cusk some other day.

You have just made two of the most common mistakes in cooking with fish—you have selected a familiar standby rather than an equally good less expensive choice, and you have failed to consider the texture the finished dish should have.

Haddock isn't a terrible choice for stew. (It's been a fish-chowder ingredient for centuries.) As long as you want a stew where the fish flakes and disintegrates somewhat, haddock works well. However, if you are aiming for a stew with firm chunks of fish, cusk would be a better choice. Cusk has a denser texture than haddock; when it is simmered, it stays intact, rather than falling apart.

When you're debating what type of fish to buy, first think about the ideal flavor and texture the finished dish should have and then—and only then—select your fish. Many fish have similar flavors and textures and are interchangeable in recipes. If you have questions about substitutions, your fishmonger should be able to answer your questions.

There's a fish to match every style of cooking. If you want a soft-textured fish to sauté and serve with a browned butter sauce, flounder works nicely. For barbecuing, choose a firm-textured steak fish such as halibut or swordfish that won't fall apart on the grill. The strong flavors of mackerel or bluefish mellow when they're marinated in a tart sauce. Monkfish is a good choice for braised dishes where a firm-textured fish is a necessity.

If you haven't eaten much fish, start out with a white-fleshed variety such as halibut, which has a delicate flavor, rather than a fish such as bluefish, which has a darker flesh and a more distinctive flavor. Swordfish is a good choice for first-time fish eaters because the texture of its flesh is more like meat than fish. (People who don't like most fish usually will eat swordfish.) Once you become accustomed to eating fish, then I think you'll appreciate the species with a stronger fish flavor such as tuna, bluefish, and salmon.

Remember that the size of a fish has nothing to do with its tenderness. Some people think that when a fish is larger, it's tougher, but that's a fallacy. I can fillet a thirty-five-pound cod and it will be just as tender cooked as a three-pound cod.

We stock more than thirty kinds of fish and shellfish at Legal Sea Foods' fish markets and restaurants. Some are seasonal specialties, while others are available the year round. With few exceptions, the fish come from North Atlantic waters, where I believe the most flavorful fish in the world originates. These are the fish I know, and these are the fish I'll discuss in this book. If you have a favorite fish I don't mention, determine what kind of texture and flavor it has, and substitute it in our recipes. Mako shark, for example, works well in the swordfish recipes, while tilefish, sea perch, and sea trout are excellent substitutes for white-fleshed fish such as cod or wolffish.

I'll tell you what I think is important about each variety, and explain about the flavor and texture of each type of fish, so you'll be better equipped to make an informed choice at the market.

Bass

Like sole, the term bass covers many different kinds of fish, including both saltwater and freshwater types. All bass have dense, tender flesh and delicate, fresh flavors. We sell only saltwater bass at Legal Sea Foods, so I'll concentrate on these varieties.

The most common bass is sea bass, also known as black bass or blackfish. Black bass, which is often used in Chinese cooking, is an excellent choice as a steamed fish. Served with a ginger-and-soy-sauce dip it is a real treat.

Bass is delicious cooked just about any way. It has a dense texture that is a little less firm than halibut (although halibut is more flaky). I like it stuffed and baked, broiled, sautéed, steamed, or poached. You can even grill bass because its texture holds up to this method of cooking.

Many people are fond of the subtle flavor of striped bass, but it has been removed from the market in many states because of the danger of the fish retaining PCBs from pollutants. (Many of the sites in America where striped bass spawn contain high levels of chemical pollutants.) Government officials with whom I've recently met say that much of the problem has been cleared up, but it will be years before striped bass will be available in quantities similar to those of the past. Also, in most states striped bass is sold only under strict regulations. In Massachusetts, for example, striped bass must be at least 34 inches long before it can be sold—which is an attempt to allow the younger fish time to grow.

I look forward to the time when we can serve striped bass frequently at our restaurants, because it is among the best-tasting species in the ocean, with a delicate fresh flavor and firm texture.

Bluefish

Every once in a while, I'll take a morning off and go fishing for bluefish, one of the great game fish of North America. Bluefish travel in schools searching for their feed of other fish such as mackerel. Once they start eating, the blues go into frenzies, leaving a trail of blood and gore wherever they've dined. Blues hit hard and keep fighting. Perhaps it's that combative energy that gives bluefish its somewhat strong flavor—I find that people either like bluefish or hate it. One reason people dislike bluefish is that too often it is not filleted immediately after being caught, and the oil-gland flavor seeps into the flesh. Quickly filleted and properly cared for, bluefish is delicious, with a tender flesh and a distinctive flavor. Bluefish has the added advantage of being an excellent source of the omega-3 fatty acids that reduce the formation of blood clots and help lower blood cholesterol levels.

Bluefish's distinctive flavor is accentuated by curing with a hot smoking process. Our bluefish pâté made from hot smoked bluefish is one of the most popular appetizers at Legal Sea Foods.

I like bluefish broiled, grilled—or oven-steamed with fresh vegetables. But it is also tasty baked with a mustard sauce.

Cod

Cod has always been one of the most popular fish in New England—and one of the most plentiful. Many a colonial fortune was made selling salted cod to other parts of the world during the early slave-trade days. Cod was so important to the New England economy that back in 1784 a carved wooden statue of the "sacred cod" was hung at the state house in Massachusetts.

The cod belongs to a family containing more than fifty species of fish, which include haddock, cusk, and pollock. Cod can grow to more than 200 pounds, although the average size is less than 25 pounds. (Small cod that weigh between 1½ and 2½ pounds are marketed as scrod.)

Cod has a white flesh, delicate flavor, and a tender, somewhat flaky texture that many people prefer. Its flesh is less firm than that of haddock and cusk.

I like cod cooked just about every way, including broiled—even though it tends to fall apart because of its flaky texture.

Cusk

I've always thought that if cusk had a more attractive name, it would be a more popular fish. Cusk tastes good and is priced right, but the word cusk sounds abrasive . . . almost unpleasant. Cusk is white-fleshed fish with a flavor similar to cod. Its firm flesh makes it a good chowder choice, but it is also delicious fried, steamed, or broiled.

Knowledgeable cooks always remove cusk's skin before serving because it is very tough, and remove the strip of bones that runs along the center of the fillet. Cusk is a dense-textured fish, so it will take longer than a fish such as haddock to cook through.

Flounder

Flounder is a generic term for any number of saltwater fish, including gray sole, dabs, flukes, and lemon sole. Their names vary, but what they all have in common is that they are flatfish. To add to the confusion, most "sole" sold in this country—such as lemon and gray sole—is really flounder. Most flounders have a delicate flavor and texture, although their thickness varies somewhat depending upon the species. I like flounder sautéed, deep-fried, or steamed. Be sure to read the section on sole for additional information. Remember that the recipes for flounder and sole are interchangeable.

Haddock

Along with cod, haddock is the most popular fish we stock. When I first opened Legal Sea Foods, haddock was among the least expensive fish we sold, but the Russians just about depleted the haddock supply when they overfished Georges Bank before the two-hundred-mile limit was set. Now, haddock runs two or three times the price of cod.

Because haddock is in short supply, the government has imposed restrictions on its sale, making it illegal to catch haddock during the spawning season. Since this restriction went into effect, a greater supply of haddock has returned to the marketplace, but it will be years before the supply is anything like what it used to be.

Haddock is a magnificent fish. It is popular because it has a very mild, pleasant flavor, a beautiful white color, and a medium-firm texture. It's possible to fillet the fish and make it virtually boneless, an advantage for people who dislike eating bony fish. I like haddock grilled, baked, and fried—all ways are equally good—but my favorite way is broiled with a little bit of butter on top.

Halibut

Halibut is a member of the flounder family even though it doesn't look it. Like flounder, when a halibut is first born its eyes are on both sides of its head, but as the halibut matures, the eyes move to the top of its head so that it can watch out for enemies as it swims along the ocean floor. I've always found it fascinating that halibut, like other flounder, have a dark upper side and a white lower side which helps them blend into their environment.

I've bought halibut that weighed almost three hundred pounds, although they usually weigh in between fifty and two hundred pounds. Because they're so large and firm-fleshed, halibut are usually cut into steaks, which makes them an excellent choice for grilling. Halibut grilled Cajun style is one of our best-selling dishes. I like halibut broiled or grilled—or even sautéed. If you're looking for a fish that holds together well, and has bones that are easy to see, halibut is a good choice.

Mackerel

Mackerel is among the most prolific fish in the ocean, and certainly ranks among the most beautiful, with its glistening blue-black skin. It is dark-fleshed fish, with a strong "fishy" flavor that marries well with a tart sauce or marinade. Europeans know this, and often marinate mackerel in acidic wine or tomato sauces, which temper its strong flavor. When mackerel is fresh, its flesh when cooked is nice and white—not as white as haddock or codfish, but much whiter than bluefish, for example. As mackerel is a fatty fish, it should be eaten as fresh as possible. (Fatty fish spoils faster than leaner fish.)

But the most important news about mackerel is how good it is for your health. Medical researchers have been studying fish oils and have discovered that mackerel is one of the most healthful fish to eat; it is loaded with the omega-3 fatty acids that help reduce the formation of blood clots and help prevent heart attacks. However, its strong flavor deters many people, and as a result, mackerel remains one of the least expensive fish to buy. Be smart. If you eat mackerel frequently, you not only save money, you do great things for your body.

One hint. Mackerel has a small bone in the middle of the fillets; be sure to have the fishmonger remove it for you.

At our restaurants we serve mackerel broiled or grilled, but I've included recipes for marinated mackerel, which has the advantage of staying in good condition for several days in the refrigerator. When you broil the fish at home, place it skin side down and top with a little butter before broiling.

Monkfish

We were among the first restaurants in the United States to start using monkfish, often called the poor man's lobster because of its similar texture and mild flavor. Monkfish are ugly creatures, of which only the tail portions are used, although most of their weight is in their heads. (A monkfish may weigh in at fifteen to twenty pounds, but only the three or four pounds of tail meat will be eaten.) In France, monkfish is known as lotte, and is one of the most expensive fish to buy. The French lotte has a whiter color than the monkfish we find in North Atlantic waters, but the texture of both species is similar.

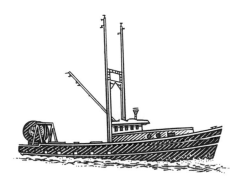

Monkfish are what we call an incidental catch, which means they don't run in schools like haddock or cod, and the fishermen can count on only what they're lucky enough to catch.

Monkfish is the most firm-textured of all fish, with a mild flavor that makes it adaptable for any number of recipes. You can slice monkfish thin and deep-fry the pieces, quickly sauté them with vegetables, or cube the fish for skewering to make kabobs. It is also good poached or braised in fish stock. We always include some monkfish in our fish chowder.

Pollock

At one time or another, practically every food writer in America has written an article about the virtues of pollock. (Someone even nicknamed pollock "Boston bluefish" to increase its appeal, but the name never caught on.) It is a tasty, slightly coarse-textured fish, with a dark-hued flesh that turns white when cooked—just the kind of fish you would expect to rival haddock in popularity. I suspect the reason pollock has not caught on is that it must be absolutely fresh to taste good. Pollock spoils more rapidly than most fish and, unfortunately, many fishmongers sell it too late. When pollock is fresh, the fillets are bright and shiny; when it is on the verge of spoiling, the fillets are dull and have a noxious odor. Pollock is one of the least expensive fish to buy, which certainly should appeal to anyone on a budget.

Fresh pollock is an excellent choice for fish and chips, chowder—or practically any type of cooking. Just make sure it is super fresh, and I'm sure you'll discover what good eating pollock can be.

Salmon

Salmon are regarded as one of the world's prime game fish, but what you see at the fishmarket is most likely a farmed product. One of the major revolutions in the fish industry has been the introduction of superior-quality farmed salmon, particularly from Scotland and Norway. Rapid air transportation has made distances meaningless. I've had salmon arrive from Norway that was so well packed that the ice hadn't even begun to melt.

I have visited a fish farm in Scotland, where the fish are first hatched, and then raised in enormous Fiberglas tanks in which both the water quality and temperature are carefully controlled. Even the food is computed scientifically. As the salmon get larger, they are transferred to new tanks where eventually they grow to as much as two feet long. The Norwegians operate a little differently; rather than using tanks, they raise salmon behind nets placed in fjords.

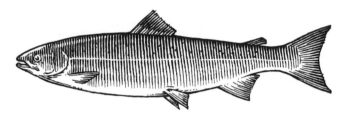

Regardless of the method used to raise the fish, the color of the farmed salmon varies considerably. The type of feed they receive is a factor in setting the depth of color. Salmon with a high fat content are lighter-colored than leaner salmon. (Also their color varies with their stage in the spawning cycle. Just before spawning, the flesh becomes paler and less flavorful.)

Many chefs still believe that wild salmon have a more distinctive flavor and are preferable for cooking. The fact is, however, that these salmon are scarce and expensive, and the farmed salmon are good substitutes. The important consideration is that the salmon be really fresh.

In addition to salmon from Scotland and Norway, we stock Coho salmon and king salmon from the West Coast. The Coho salmon we get are small-sized, with a medium texture, and a more delicate flavor than most other types. Coho salmon are tasty butterflied and broiled or stuffed whole and baked.

I think salmon is delicious either grilled or broiled, although some people prefer it poached and served with green mayonnaise. At the restaurants we either grill or broil king salmon steaks. Salmon is an excellent source of the omega-3 fatty acids that help prevent cholesterol and reduce the formation of blood clots.

Scrod

There's no such fish as scrod. Scrod is a nickname given to haddock or cod that weigh less than 2½ pounds. When it is sold at the Boston fish auction, the auctioneer calls out, "We have a trip of scrod/cod or scrod/haddock." Generally, there is little difference in the taste, but the texture varies. Some of the larger fish are flakier. I prefer a thicker cut of scrod because it retains more flavor.

Both cod and haddock are mild-flavored, white-fleshed fish, which means scrod also has a pleasant, mild flavor and a somewhat flaky texture.

Scrod is delicious cooked practically any way. I like it broiled, grilled, baked, sautéed, or steamed.

Shad Roe

Shad is a coastal fish that comes into the warmer waters of rivers to spawn. It has a delicious flavor, but is too bony for most people to enjoy, although it is possible to find shad fillets in some markets. (If you are fortunate enough to track down shad fillets, just dip them in flour, sauté them quickly in butter, and serve with a slice of lemon to squeeze on top. Any more complicated sauce would overpower the delicate taste.)

Shad, however, contributes one of the great delicacies of regional American cooking—shad roe, available fresh in many parts of the country during the early spring.

The roe are bigger than you might expect—anywhere from five to six inches long, two to three inches wide, and about one inch thick. When you buy the roe, the double sac of eggs will be covered with a membrane, also forming the connective tissue. Try not to pierce the membrane, or the eggs will splatter all over the pan while cooking.

A traditional method for cooking roe is to broil it with bacon, but I think this tends to dry it out. An easier way is to slowly sauté the roe in butter or bacon fat, and serve with lemon. As the roe may splatter while cooking, cover it with the lid to a steamer pot, which cuts down on the grease while allowing the steam to escape.

Sole

Many people call all flatfish sole—but that is not accurate. The true sole is the Dover sole, sometimes imported into this country from England, but in the United States the members of the sole family are all flounder—regardless of what they're called. Both sole and flounder are members of the flatfish family, but the difference lies in their body shapes; sole is deeper-bodied with a more elliptical shape, while flounder has a more rounded body.

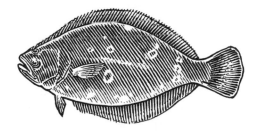

The most expensive "soles" are gray and lemon sole. Gray sole has the most delicate texture and flavor in the flounder family, while the texture and flavor of lemon sole are coarser. You will pay twice as much money for either gray or lemon sole as you will for dab, yellowtail flounder, or blackback flounder.

Most fish markets sell yellowtail flounder, fluke, dab, and other flatfish—sometimes labeled flounder, sometimes sole. These are different species of flatfish and they all have their own peculiarities. Sole is one of the strangest of fish. It starts life with eyes on either side of its head, but as it begins to grow, the eyes move sideways to the same side of the head. As the fish swims along the bottom of the ocean, both eyes are looking up.

The tendency of fishmongers to lump together all members of

the flatfish family under the generic label of sole generates a great deal of confusion on the part of the consumer. In general, sole has a delicate flavor and texture, although its thickness varies considerably, depending upon the species. (Some days sole is half an inch thick; other days, one inch.)

Although sole is usually sautéed or baked, you can also broil it, as long as you keep basting it.

Swordfish

There's nothing better than a piece of charcoal-grilled swordfish. Many fish taste delicious grilled, but swordfish tastes best because its unique flavor is accentuated by the grilling process.

Swordfish meat is usually cut into steaks, which is the easiest way to deal with the huge fish, which weigh between two hundred and six hundred pounds. Some unscrupulous vendors will sell mako shark as swordfish. A swordfish steak has whorls (a pattern in the flesh that resembles the cross section of a tree) which the mako shark lacks. Mako shark also has skin that feels like sandpaper when you rub it against the grain.

Sportsmen know swordfish as great game fish. They're speedy, and feisty when caught. Commercial fishermen in this area harpoon swordfish. These are the best-quality fish and we pay a premium price for them. The Japanese run miles of line with hooks and barbs attached to floating barrels to catch these elusive fish.

The flesh is dense and reddish-colored, turning almost beige when cooked. Swordfish is a very versatile fish. We serve it grilled (both as steaks and kabobs), broiled, but it is also tasty sautéed or baked. For a while, Americans shunned swordfish because of a fear of mercury poisoning, but later testing showed the danger to have abated, and swordfish has taken its rightful place as one of America's most popular fish.

Tuna

Most Americans have eaten canned tuna—but rarely have they tried this fish fresh. Consumption of canned tuna is so high that experts estimate that canned tuna constitutes one fourth of all the seafood eaten in the United States.

People are just beginning to realize that fresh tuna is also delicious. Tuna is a member of the same fish family as mackerel, which means it also is dark-fleshed and oily, but with a firmer-textured flesh. When you buy tuna, only purchase pieces that are a reddish color (brown color is a sure sign that the fish has been in the display case too long). When the fish is cooked, the flesh turns brown.

I like tuna broiled, grilled, or baked. Leftover tuna is delicious flaked or sliced up in main-course salads.

Wolffish

Wolffish, sometimes known as ocean catfish, is delicious eating. It has firm white flesh that is somewhat flaky, and a sweet, mild flavor. It's a good thing wolffish is so tasty, because it is one of the ugliest species of fish to swim in the ocean. The wolffish is so called because it has teeth that appear animal-like. In fact, wolffish is so ugly that before it is even sent to the wholesale fish vendors, the heads are removed.

I like wolffish baked, oven-steamed, fried, or broiled.

Basic Techniques
for Cooking Fish

No matter how many new recipes we add to our Legal Sea Foods menu, fish cooked simply remains the number one choice of our customers. They recognize, as we do, that when fish is fresh, there's no need for fancy sauces or other frills. I think a piece of fresh fish that's broiled—or baked—and served with a touch of butter or lemon juice is true gourmet food in the best sense of the word.

Starting with fresh fish, however, is only half the story. The best fish in the world, poorly cooked, will be ruined. Scrod that's baked in a preheated oven at the right temperature until it is just cooked through will be moist and flavorful. The same scrod, placed in the same oven and baked fifteen minutes too long will come out dry and tasteless. The important factor in cooking fish is not the method you use, but rather the care with which you cook it.

Our restaurants are stocked with special grills for charbroiling, huge machines for steaming fish, and gas convection ovens that reach temperatures unobtainable with home equipment. Don't expect to duplicate these restaurant conditions at home. In addition, some recipes we feature are difficult to prepare successfully in a home kitchen. Were you to try our pan-blackened halibut, for example, you would end up with an acrid, smoky smell throughout your house because using this cooking technique requires powerful vents, such as those found in our restaurants, which immediately suck away smoke and odors. For the most part, however, there's no reason why you can't prepare fish that's the equal of that found at Legal Sea Foods. All you need is a source for quality fresh fish and attention to detail when cooking.

The most common mistake people make in cooking fish is to treat it like meat. Meat flesh is composed of long bundles of muscle and connective tissue and often needs to be pounded or cooked for a long time with moist heat in order to be tender.

Fish, on the other hand, is naturally tender. Unlike meat, the muscles and connective tissue of fish are formed in short fibers rather than long bundles. In addition, fish contains considerably less connective tissue than meat. This means there's no need to cook fish for a long time to tenderize it. Fish flesh is tender before it is cooked and remains tender when it is properly cooked.

For all these reasons, fish should be cooked only to the point when it's done. Once fish is cooked past this critical point the tissue in the flesh dries out. You cannot make fish more tender by overcooking it, but you can make it dry or tasteless.

Fish, similar to meat, continues to cook slightly after it is removed from the heat. For best results, regardless of the cooking method, you should cook fish just until it has lost its translucency and turned opaque—and no longer. Do not test fish for doneness by waiting until the flesh flakes when tested with a fork. Fish cooked to this point is overcooked.

Overcooked fish is a disaster. When people tell me they dislike fish, I suspect they probably have spent a lifetime eating overcooked fish, and really don't know how delicious properly prepared fish tastes. If you tend to overcook fish, buy fish such as cod, which is thicker, rather than a flatfish such as sole, which cooks almost immediately. Frankly, I prefer to eat a thicker piece of fish because I think it retains more flavor.

Fish should be served the minute it is cooked. At our restaurants the fish is rushed to the table rather than allowed to sit under a heat lamp, losing flavor and drying up by the minute while the waiter scrambles to assemble an order. The same principle applies at home. Plan your meal so that everything is ready to serve when the fish comes off the stove.

Fish is so tender, and cooks so rapidly, that there's no need for microwave cooking to save time. Regardless of the cooking method, most fish can be cooked in a period of five to thirty minutes. Deep-fried oysters or clams cook in about a minute, while even a large salmon takes no longer than thirty to forty minutes to poach.

When you're in doubt about how long to cook a piece of fish, follow the rule of thumb devised by the Canadian Department of Fisheries. After extensive testing the department found that regardless of the cooking method or the type of fish, by measuring the fish at its thickest point it was possible to pinpoint the

ideal cooking time. The department determined that ten minutes' cooking time for each inch of thickness worked out about
right. The cooking temperature would be the same for broiled,
fried, poached, or steamed fish, but if you are baking fish be sure
to do it at a high temperature, about 450 degrees. This method
works whether the fish is whole, cut into fillets, or left in steaks.

If you live in an area where it's impossible to buy fresh fish and
frozen fish is your only option, choose recipes where you can
cook the fish while it is still frozen. Fish loses about 30 percent of
its moisture as it thaws, including a significant amount of the
water-soluble vitamins and minerals.

At Legal Sea Foods you can buy fish fried, baked, broiled,
grilled, poached, sautéed, or even steamed. We use all these
methods because the way fish is prepared is so often a matter of
personal preference. I eat fish at least seven or eight times a
week—sometimes twice a day. Some days I might prefer haddock steamed with a few vegetables; other times I'll be in the
mood for baked haddock with tomatoes and cheese or fried
haddock with chips. Most fish are so versatile that you can cook
them in any way, while a few fish taste best if prepared with a
specific technique. In the preceding chapter when I described
the individual types of fish we serve, I mentioned my favorite
ways to cook each kind of fish. Start, however, by mastering the
basic cooking techniques I explain in this chapter and you'll be
able to cook any fish in the ocean.

Baking

Most fish responds well to baking. If the fish is fatty, such as
salmon or bluefish, there's little need for additional fat. A leaner
fish, such as cod, would need a dot of butter or oil.

You'll notice that the baking recipes in this book call for an
oven temperature of 400 to 450 degrees F., which is a higher
temperature than you might expect. When I started out in the
restaurant business, I baked fish at high temperatures out of
necessity (lower temperatures take twice as long) and discovered to my delight that fish baked rapidly stays moist because the
high heat seals in the juices.

For plain baked fish, place it in a buttered pan, or in a pan strewn with vegetables for flavor, and dot it with butter. If you wish, add 1/4 to 1/2 cup of white wine to baste the fish as it bakes. (If you use wine, be sure to put the fish in an enamel or stainless steel pan because the wine would react to an aluminum pan, giving an off taste to the cooking juices.) Count on about 10 minutes cooking time per pound of fish. The fish will be done when it loses its translucency and turns opaque. Serve immediately.

Baked Scrod

> 2 tablespoons butter
> 2 pounds scrod fillets
> Lemon wedges

Preheat the oven to 425 degrees. Butter a large baking dish and place the fillets in the dish, skin side down. Dot the fish with butter, and bake for about 10 minutes. Baste occasionally with the cooking juices if you wish. The cooking time depends upon the thickness of the fish. Remove the fish from the heat and serve with lemon wedges. (Serves 4)

Broiling

All fish can be broiled, as long as a few rules are followed. Preheat the broiler; give the fish a protective coating with oil; and cook it the proper distance from the heat.

Years ago I devised what I believe to be the best way of broiling fish—a method so successful that Julia Child mentioned it in one of her books. Forget anything you have ever read about broiling fish a set amount of time on each side. Broiled fish should be cooked on only one side because the radiant heat from the pan will cook the other side. My method was born of necessity because the only kind of fish that can be turned successfully is steak fish such as swordfish or salmon. All other fish will fall apart in the process.

Coating the fish with a flavorless oil before broiling is important because it protects the surface from burning and retains the moisture in the fish. If you're on a diet, and don't want to use oil, I suggest you bake or steam the fish, rather than broiling it.

How close you place the fish to the broiling surface depends upon how hot the broiler has become. Three to four inches away is ideal.

I'm giving you the basic technique for broiling fish, using haddock as the example. This is one of the perennial favorites at our restaurants. You can even broil a thin flatfish such as flounder using this technique, but watch carefully, or it will dry out.

Broiled Haddock

> 2 pounds haddock fillets
> 2 tablespoons flavorless oil, such as Wesson
> Freshly ground pepper
> Butter

Preheat the broiler at least 20 minutes before you plan to cook the fish. Dry the fish with paper towels, coat both sides with the oil, and place in a broiler pan. Broil the fish about 3 to 4 inches below the cooking element until cooked through. Fillets 1 inch thick should be done in 8 to 10 minutes. Dot the fish with butter just before serving. (Serves 4)

VARIATION: *Broiled Cod with Bread or Cracker Crumbs.* When the fish is just about cooked through, lightly sprinkle the surface with 2–3 tablespoons of crumbs, and place the fish back under the broiler long enough to brown the crumbs.

Frying

Frying is one of the most tasty ways to prepare fish, but you must start with absolutely fresh cooking fat heated to the correct temperature. When you try to save money by reusing fat several times, your fish will have an off flavor—and will burn more easily. If your cooking temperature is too low, the fish coating will absorb fat and the fish will taste greasy; if the temperature is too high, the coating will burn, and the fish may not cook through, depending upon its density. I prefer to fry fish in fat heated to 365 degrees. If you are going to fry fish, you should buy a deep-fat thermometer and test the fat with it frequently.

The fat you use should be as flavorless as possible so that the true flavor of the fish comes through. We're continuously testing cooking fats and have settled upon a pure vegetable shortening with no additives as the choice that interferes with the flavor of the fish the least. We use a commercial variety that's similar to Crisco. A cooking oil such as Wesson would also be satisfactory.

At Legal, we dip all food to be fried first in buttermilk and then in a special corn-flour mix, Flour Mix for Fried Fish. Of course, you could use milk, but I think the buttermilk adds a richer flavor. We then shake off any excess mix and deep-fry the fish in preheated fat until it is cooked through but not overdone. It's important to fry the fish a few pieces at a time so the pan does not get overcrowded. If it does, the fish tend to stick together and don't cook evenly.

Some people prefer to dip fish in a wet batter and then fry it (as do the English with their fish and chips), but I believe this method makes fish greasy. I've tried many a wet batter and have always come back to soaking the fish in buttermilk and then coating the pieces with a dry mixture. I also think a wet batter tends to make the individual fish pieces stick together.

A piece of fish fried with a dry batter will be crisp, not greasy. The fish steams in its own juices, which the batter seals in, and the flavor is retained. Serve fried fish immediately, or the steam exuded from the interior will make the coating soggy.

Fried Pollock

I've selected pollock for this basic recipe, although you could use practically any fish. Haddock, cod, or cusk are favored by many restaurants, but if the fish isn't specified on the menu, it's often pollock, whose price is far lower than the better-known varieties. Be sure to serve the fish with a good-quality tartar sauce. We take great pride in our sauce and consider it almost as important as the fish.

3 cups vegetable shortening
Buttermilk for dipping
About 1 cup Flour Mix for Fried Fish

2 pounds pollock, cut into serving pieces
Tartar Sauce
Lemon wedges

Heat the fat in a heavy, deep pot until it reaches a temperature of 365 degrees. Meanwhile dip the pollock first in buttermilk, and then in the flour mix. Shake to remove any excess coating, and place on a dish next to the stove.

Test the fat with a deep-fat thermometer to make sure it is hot enough, and fry the pollock, a few pieces at a time, until cooked through and crispy. A piece of pollock about 1 inch thick will be ready in 2 to 3 minutes. The fish pieces are best served the moment they are cooked, but you can hold them on a serving platter until they are all done, if you prefer. Serve with Tartar Sauce and garnish with lemon wedges.

VARIATIONS:

Fried Clams. Shuck the clams and follow the cooking directions above, making sure not to crowd the pan. The clams will cook through in about 1 minute.

Fried Soft-Shell Crabs. This is one of the best ways to enjoy soft-shell crabs. Follow the directions for cleaning (See Index) and the directions for cooking above. The crabs will cook through in approximately 2 minutes.

Fried Oysters. Shuck the oysters and follow the cooking directions above. The oysters will cook through in about 1 minute.

Fried Shrimp. Peel the shrimp and follow the cooking directions above. The shrimp will cook through in about 1 to 1½ minutes, depending upon their size.

Grilling

Grilling is one of the most popular cooking techniques we use at the restaurants, but we have a much different setup from the one you have at home. Our restaurants are equipped with huge gas grills manned by grill men who can tell just by looking at fish when it is cooked through. A good grill man can look at the flame and decide where to place the fish. Once it is seared, he shifts it to a cooler spot to finish cooking.

You can accomplish the same thing at home by moving the fish to the edge of the grill, where the temperature is lower.

Firm-textured fish cut into steaks—or whole fish—are the best choices for grilling because they hold together better during cooking. Fillets would fall apart as you tried to turn them over. If you have a thick whole fish, slash it twice diagonally across its body so that the heat can penetrate more evenly. When I charcoal-grill a whole haddock, for example, I prepare it in this manner.

Oil the fish with a flavorless vegetable oil before you put it on the grill. Sear it in the hottest part of the grill, then move it to the edges to continue cooking. Turn the fish once. Serve immediately.

Grilled Halibut

Halibut is ideal for grilling because it can be cut like a steak, has a firm texture, and doesn't fall apart as you move it.

    3 tablespoons vegetable oil
    2 pounds halibut steaks
    Cayenne pepper
    Freshly ground black pepper
    2 tablespoons butter (optional)

Oil the halibut and season it with a dash of cayenne pepper and some black pepper. Let the halibut marinate while you prepare the grill. Use whichever type of grill you prefer, but if you are using a charcoal grill, make sure that the flames have died down and the coals are glowing before you cook the fish.

Sear the fish on both sides, then let it cook through in a cooler spot. Dot with butter before serving.

Poaching

Poaching a whole fish, or large pieces of fish, is an excellent way to preserve the moisture—particularly if the fish is going to be served cold.

A fish poacher is a useful piece of equipment to own, but you can improvise with a large, deep pan—such as a turkey roaster—and a meat rack.

You can poach fish either in salted water or in a flavored broth. Frankly, I can discern very little difference in flavor—if any—from using a broth, but many people swear by a flavored court bouillon. Either way, you should wrap the fish in cheesecloth, place it on the rack, and lower it into the preheated liquid. There should be just enough liquid to cover the fish. The water should be at a gentle boil.

Poach the fish about 10 minutes per pound, but check after 8 minutes so that you don't overcook it. If you wish to cool the fish in the liquid, slightly undercook it because it will continue to cook as the liquid cools.

Poached salmon is a traditional New England dish for July Fourth, but if you prefer you can substitute striped bass—or black bass.

Poached Salmon

 1 4-pound salmon, scaled
 Cheesecloth
 Water
 3 tablespoons salt
 2 tablespoons white vinegar

Keep the head and tail on the salmon. Cut a piece of cheesecloth about a foot or so longer than the fish. Lay it out on the counter, and place the fish lengthwise in the center of the cloth. Wrap the cloth around the fish and tie it securely with string at each end. This will leave the ends of the cheesecloth free, to either tie the fish to the rack to keep it from floating to the surface or to be used as handles to lift from the water.

Place the fish on a rack, and loosely tie the cheesecloth wrapping to the rack to prevent the fish from floating to the surface of the water as it cooks. Bring the water in the poacher to a boil. Add the salt and vinegar. Place the fish in the pan. The boiling water should cover the fish by about 1 inch. When the water returns again to a simmer, reduce the heat and poach the fish for about 10 minutes per inch thickness of fish.

Remove the fish from the water, drain it for about 2 minutes, then remove the strings and cheesecloth, rolling the fish out onto a platter. Using a small, sharp knife, remove the skin from the gills to the tail. Serve with Easy Blender Mayonnaise or a watercress or egg sauce. (Serves 6)

Sautéing

Sautéing is an excellent method for cooking thin fish fillets or whole flatfish. It is important to sauté fish in a large pan that is heavy enough to distribute the heat evenly. A thick iron pan is ideal.

When you sauté fish, melt enough butter (or butter and oil) so that the bottom of the pan is generously coated. Make sure the fat is hot before you add the coated fish or it will stick to the pan. Arrange the fish in the pan, leaving plenty of space between the fillets. Keep the pan uncovered, otherwise the fish will steam rather than fry, and the coating will be soggy rather than crisp. Sauté the fillets until they are a light golden color on each side, turning once. Serve immediately.

Sautéed Sole or Flounder

> 5 tablespoons butter
> 2 tablespoons light vegetable oil
> 2 pounds sole or flounder fillets
> Buttermilk, for dipping
> Flour, for dredging
> Lemon slices

Heat the butter and oil in a large frying pan until hot. Dip the fish first in buttermilk, then in flour, shaking to remove any excess flour.

Sauté the fish for 2 to 3 minutes on each side, depending upon the thickness of the fish. Remove and serve with lemon wedges. (Serves 4)

VARIATIONS:

Sole with Browned Butter. After the fish is done, place it on a hot serving dish and keep warm. Clean out the pan and add about 4 tablespoons of butter (1 tablespoon for each serving of fish). Cook the butter over medium-high heat until it is lightly browned. Pour it over the fish and garnish with the lemon wedges.

Sole with Herbs and Butter. Follow the directions above, but add chopped chives and parsley—or chopped sweet marjoram or chervil to the butter. Sauté the herbs with the butter for 30 seconds, then pour the herb butter over the fish before serving.

Oven Steaming

I've been cooking fish this way for years. Oven steaming fish is easy to do and is a particularly useful cooking technique for people who work.

Essentially, you steam the fish along with thinly sliced vegetables in an envelope of heavy aluminum foil. This technique allows the fish to steam in its own juices. You can add herbs, butter, or cheese—and make the recipe as fancy or plain as you wish. The nice thing about this method is that the fish always comes out moist, and there are plenty of fish and vegetable juices to spoon over a baked potato or rice. There is a wonderful aroma when you open the packet—and the bonus is that fish cooked this way is almost as good served cold or reheated.

Steamed Cod with Vegetables

This is one of the first dishes we served at the restaurant when we started out. It's almost a national dish because no matter what section of the country you come from, you can use a local fish and the vegetables of the season. I vary both the fish and vegetables. Sometimes I use broccoli and mushrooms, other times thinly sliced string beans, tomatoes, or summer squash—or a combination of all three. Whichever vegetables you use, slice them no wider than 1/4 inch thick so that they will cook as fast as the fish.

2 pounds cod fillets
6 ounces broccoli, sliced 1/4 inch thick
4 ounces sliced mushrooms
1 tablespoon minced fresh basil, sweet marjoram, or
  lovage
Salt
Freshly ground black pepper
1 tablespoon butter

Preheat the oven to 450 degrees. Cut the aluminum foil large enough to hold the fish and vegetables. Place the fish in the middle of the foil, and cover with the broccoli, mushrooms, and basil. Add salt and pepper to taste, then dot with the butter.

Make an envelope out of the foil, enclosing the fish and vegetables, and place it on a cookie sheet. Bake for about 15 minutes. The fish will be cooked through, and the vegetables will retain some of their crunch. (Serves 4)

Traditional Steamed Fish

If you wish to steam fish the traditional way, it is important to purchase a good-quality steamer at a restaurant-supply store. The little racks that you can buy for a few dollars at the hardware store never work out well; it is worth it to invest in a regular steamer.

Place about 1 inch of water in the bottom of the pot. I like to add a teaspoon of soy sauce because it adds flavor without changing the basic taste of the fish. Bring the water to a boil, insert the steamer basket holding the fish, cover, and steam until the fish is barely cooked through. Steamed fish cooks faster than you might expect. Thin fillets are cooked through in 2 to 3 minutes, while a piece of fish 1 inch thick will take 8 to 10 minutes. Remember that the density of the flesh also counts. Monkfish or cusk, which are densely fleshed fish, take longer to steam than haddock or sole.

Let the fish sit for a moment before serving.

Cleaning and Filleting Fish

Unless you have a fisherman in the family, it's unlikely that you'll have to clean and fillet fish. Any fishmonger should be able to perform these steps for you, but it's always useful to be familiar with the process.

Cleaning

Cut from the bottom of the fish near the anal area (the hole where the fish gets rid of waste). Cut with a sharp knife, and don't go too deep —just cut the skin. Cut all the way up to the mouth.

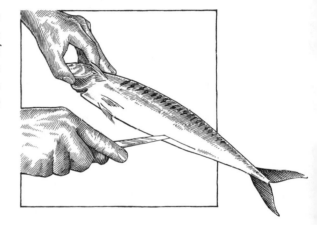

Next, remove the gills—the organs that filter the air. The gills are always found beneath the cheeks. When you lift up each cheek, the pinkish-red, spongy mass beneath is the gill. Cut around each gill and pull it out.

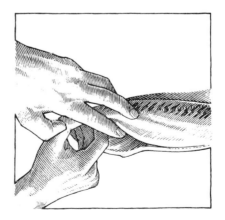

You have to be careful not to break the gall, which can give an off flavor to the fish. The gall is greenish-colored and is found right around the liver. To remove the innards of the fish, scoop your hand inside the intestine and gently dislodge it from the wall. It should come out in one piece. Rinse out the fish, and pack ice into its body cavity as well as around it.

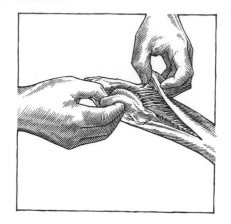

Filleting

The most important part of filleting fish is to use a sharp knife. A fish knife about twelve inches long, with a long, thin edge, is helpful. I suggest you also wear an apron because the process is sloppy. One caution: it is essential to keep the hand with which you are holding the fish away from the knife edge. Otherwise, the knife might slip and you could cut yourself badly.

The first step is to scale the fish. Take the back end of the knife and scrape off the scales. Don't apply too much pressure because the flesh is delicate and breaks easily. Restaurant-supply stores sell fish scalers, known as curry combs, named after the combs used to groom horses. Scales can't harm you, but they're unpleasant to eat. Wash the fish off after scaling it.

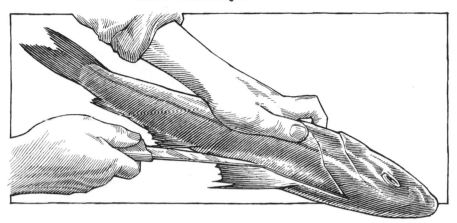

Lay the fish down so that its head faces right, with its back facing you. Take the knife and start at the head of the fish by making a diagonal cut just behind the gills. Keep the knife above the center bone so you slice only the meat, but at the same time try to feel the edge of the bone. (The closer to the center bone you stay, the more meat is going to be contained on the fillet.)

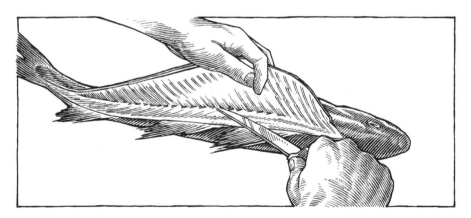

Lift up the fillet a bit and with the point of the knife, cut a little deeper along the spine. Keep cutting down until you reach the rib bones. Remember, the more often you repeat this step, the easier it gets. You should aim to lift the tip of the knife slightly so that you avoid cutting into the bones. When you reach the top of the rib cage, cut straight down to dislodge the fillet.

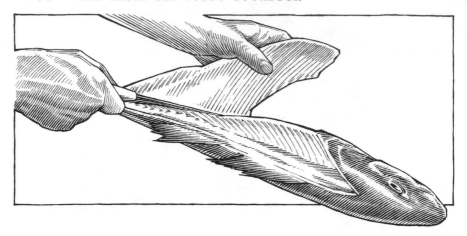

When you reach the end of the rib cage, insert the knife all the way through to dislodge the bottom third of the fillet. Cut to separate the fillet from the bone.

Now turn the fish over, placing the tail where the head once was. The spine will be facing you. (Were you to flip the fish, the stomach cavity, not the spine, would be in front.) Make a cut behind the head of the fish at the same angle you did before. Place the knife at the tail end and cut into the meat, keeping the knife close to the spine. Continue along, reversing the steps you did on the other side. When you reach the stomach cavity, lift up with your left hand and with the other hand cut down, dislodging the fillet. Continue cutting in this manner until you reach the head. You now have two fillets and a frame. If the frame is from a nonoily, white-fleshed fish, use it for stock.

Immediately place the fillets in the refrigerator or on ice.

Our Favorite Fish Recipes

About the Recipes

Fish is the original convenience food. It cooks in minutes—needing few or no embellishments to taste good. I like fish best served plain or accented by a simple sauce made with the pan juices and some fresh herbs and vegetables.

Before modern techniques made it possible to savor fish at its peak point of flavor, cooks masked the flavor of mediocre fish with heavy sauces and exotic ingredients—and called the result gourmet cooking. When fish is really fresh, there's no need to hide its flavor with elaborate sauces and ingredients.

I've selected recipes for this cookbook that are easy to prepare. I have little patience with recipes that take half a day to make (although I might enjoy eating them on occasion). If you're in a hurry, there are dozens of recipes that you can put together in less than half an hour. You'll discover most of your favorite recipes from our restaurants, as well as many others that are wonderful choices for home cooks.

Whatever the type of recipe, you should always start with the freshest fish you can find and the best ingredients you can afford. I never stint on the quality of the ingredients we use in our food, although we could certainly save money by cutting a few corners. I believe that top-quality ingredients have a cumulative effect in determining the final taste of a dish. We make the vinaigrette for our squid salad with a flavorful Chianti vinegar that Roger discovered in Italy. We could substitute an inexpensive red wine vinegar, of course, but the salad would never taste the same.

You'll notice that I rarely call for salt in these recipes, although you can add salt if you wish. I think that fish dishes don't need salt because there's enough natural salt in the fish. I also prefer to use fresh—rather than dried—herbs, because their oils add so much aroma and flavor to the completed recipe. If you don't have an herb garden, many supermarkets now stock fresh herbs the year round in the produce department, or you can buy herbs at specialty food shops.

Feel free to substitute any fish that you can find locally for those called for in these recipes. Wherever you live, there's fresh fish available if you just take the time to locate it. I've featured the saltwater fish that are plentiful in New England, but the recipes work equally well with freshwater fish—as long as you match their textures and flavors with those of the fish I suggest.

Bass

Baked Sea Bass with Herbs

Serve the bass either warm or at room temperature. The oils of the mixed fresh herbs and the lemon juice flavor the bass, while the bacon fat keeps it moist. Substitute any whole fish for the bass if you wish.

    1 3½-pound whole sea bass, cleaned
    1 tablespoon vegetable oil
    Freshly ground black pepper
    2½–3 cups mixed fresh herb stalks, such as thyme, lovage
        or celery, mint, rosemary, basil or oregano
    2 lemons, thinly sliced
    3 slices bacon
    Sprigs of mint or basil

Preheat the oven to 425 degrees. Rinse and dry the fish, and brush it with the vegetable oil. Sprinkle the skin with the pepper. Place about 1 cup of the herbs in a greased baking dish just large enough to hold the fish and herbs, and cover with the fish. Stuff the cavity of the fish with ½ cup of the herbs, and then strew the remaining herbs on top. Cover the herbs with half of the lemon slices, overlapping them if necessary. Top with the bacon.

Bake for about 12 minutes, or until cooked through. Let the fish rest in the pan for about 5 minutes before you serve it. Discard the herbs and lemon slices, skin the fish, and lift it to a platter lined with the remaining lemon slices. Garnish with the mint or basil. Serve with wedges of lemon or lime. (Serves 4)

VARIATION: *Baked Salmon with Mint or Dill.* Follow the directions above, using either mint or dill stalks rather than the mixed herbs. Substitute 1 tablespoon of butter dotted over the lemon slices for the bacon.

Grilled Striped Bass with Garlic and Basil

Striped bass tastes best with a simple sauce.

    2 pounds striped bass fillet
    3 tablespoons oil
    Juice of 1 lemon
    4 to 6 tablespoons butter
    4 cloves garlic, finely chopped
    2 tablespoons basil, finely chopped
    Dash of cayenne pepper

Marinate the fish in the oil and lemon juice for at least 30 minutes before grilling. Grill for 10 to 15 minutes, turning once. The length of time depends upon the thickness of the fillet.

Heat the butter in a saucepan and stew the garlic for about 3 minutes, stirring frequently. Do not let it brown. Add the basil and a dash of cayenne pepper. Remove the pan from the heat.

Either pour the garlic butter over the fish just before serving, or serve it in a sauceboat on the side. (Serves 4)

Bluefish

Smoked Bluefish Pâté

During my travels, I tasted a bluefish pâté I thought would be an interesting addition to our restaurant menu. After much experimenting, we came up with this version that uses a hot pressed smoked bluefish as the base. This makes a densely flavored pâté; for a lighter version, try the variation.

1 pound smoked bluefish fillets
1/4 pound cream cheese
3 tablespoons butter
2 tablespoons Cognac
1 tablespoon minced onions
1/4–1/2 teaspoon Worcestershire sauce
1 tablespoon lemon juice
Salt
Freshly ground black pepper

Purée the bluefish, cream cheese, butter, and Cognac in a food processor. Add the onions, Worcestershire sauce, and lemon juice and pulse the machine on and off until the ingredients are combined. Taste and correct the seasonings with salt and pepper.

Pack into a crock and serve with crackers or thinly sliced pieces of toast. The pâté will keep in the refrigerator for 4 to 5 days, or may be frozen for up to 3 months. (Makes about 3 1/4 cups)

VARIATION: This version uses a greater amount of cream cheese and flavorings.

1 pound smoked bluefish fillets
1/2 pound cream cheese
1/4 cup butter
3 tablespoons minced onions
2 tablespoons Cognac

2 tablespoons lemon juice
1/2 teaspoon Worcestershire sauce
Salt
Freshly ground black pepper

Prepare as above. (Makes about 4 cups)

Bluefish with Mustard Sauce

Our son Marc invented this recipe for our Chestnut Hill restaurant. It proved such a success that Roger, our oldest son, came up with his own version for the Boston restaurants he manages. Marc spreads the sauce on the raw fish and bakes it. Roger prefers to broil the fish until it is almost done, spread it with the sauce, and pop it back under the broiler to brown lightly. Either way, it's delicious. Try both ways and decide which you prefer.

MUSTARD SAUCE
1 1/2 cups mayonnaise
1/2 cup Dijon mustard
1/2 cup grated horseradish
1/4 cup minced onions
1/4 cup finely chopped parsley
Worcestershire sauce
Hot pepper sauce
2 pounds bluefish fillets

Preheat the oven to 450 degrees. Combine the mayonnaise, mustard, horseradish, onions, and parsley. Season to taste with the Worcestershire and hot pepper sauces.

If you are baking the fish, spread it generously with the mustard sauce and bake it for 15 minutes. Should you wish to broil it,

place it under a preheated broiler, and cook until almost done, about 6 minutes. Remove the fish, spread lightly with sauce, and return it under the broiler until it is lightly browned. (Serves 4)

NOTE: Any extra sauce can be stored in the refrigerator where it is delicious with fried oysters, squid—or any broiled or baked fish.

Bluefish with Citrus Juices

The rich flavor of bluefish contrasts well with this tart marinade made with orange and lemon juices. It is important to use freshly squeezed juices because refrigerated packaged juices will not produce a fresh-tasting marinade. You can substitute almost any fish fillets for the bluefish, but they should be about 1 inch thick. This dish should be chilled overnight in the refrigerator before serving to allow the flavors time to meld.

2 pounds bluefish fillets (about 1 inch thick) with skin
Flour
3/4 cup olive oil
1/2 cup freshly squeezed lemon juice
3/4 cup freshly squeezed orange, tangerine, or tangelo
   juice
1/4 teaspoon cayenne pepper
3/4 cup chopped onions (about 2)
1 red pepper, coarsely chopped
1 tablespoon finely chopped garlic
3 tablespoons chopped fresh basil *or* 2 tablespoons
   chopped coriander or mint
1 peeled orange, thinly sliced

Cut the fillets into 2-inch-wide pieces and lightly dust them with flour. Heat 1/4 cup of the oil in a large frying pan and sauté the fillets on both sides until browned and cooked through. Drain them on paper bags.

Combine the lemon juice, orange juice, cayenne pepper, the remaining oil, onions, chopped peppers, garlic, and herbs. Place the fish in a deep glass or earthenware serving dish and cover with the marinade. It may be necessary to layer the fish. If this is the case, pour some of the marinade over each layer. This amount of marinade should be sufficient to cover the fish. If it is not, press down lightly on the fish, and add a little more lemon and orange juice. Top with the orange slices.

Chill at least overnight before serving. The fish will keep in good condition for several days if stored in the refrigerator in a dish covered with foil. (Serves 4 to 6)

VARIATION: *Scrod with Citrus Juices.* Substitute scrod for the bluefish, and lime juice for the lemon juice. Add 1 small hot pepper, cut into rings.

Cod

Cod Soup

This recipe works particularly well with a flaky-fleshed fish, such as cod—although firmer-fleshed fish, such as cusk or pollock, is also good if you slice it into serving pieces before adding it to the soup. For maximum flavor, the tomatoes must be ripe. (If tomatoes are out of season, use drained canned Italian plum tomatoes.)

    1/4 cup olive oil
    3 cups coarsely chopped onions
    2 teaspoons minced garlic
    1 strip fresh orange peel, about 1 inch wide and 1 1/2
        inches long
    5 tomatoes, peeled, seeded, and chopped (about 3 cups
        pulp)
    1/4 cup dry white wine
    8 cups Fish Stock
    2 pounds cod fillets
    1 tablespoon chopped basil
    Salt and pepper

Heat the olive oil in a large stainless steel or enameled pot, and stir in the onions. Cook over medium heat for about 5 minutes, stirring occasionally, then add the garlic and orange peel. Cook another 5 minutes, then stir in the tomatoes and white wine.

Simmer for 10 minutes, stirring occasionally, and add the Fish Stock.

Simmer the tomato mixture and stock for about 20 minutes so that the flavors meld. Add the fish and simmer 10 minutes longer, or just until the fish is cooked through. About 3 minutes before serving, add the basil. Taste and season with salt and pepper. Remove the orange rind before serving. (Serves 4 to 6)

VARIATION: *Fish Soup with Red Pepper Garlic Sauce.* For a heartier version add 2 cups thinly sliced potatoes along with the stock, and stir a spoonful of Red Pepper Sauce into the soup before serving.

See *Steamed Cod with Vegetables* (in the Index).
See also scrod listings in the Index.

Cusk

Spicy Fried Cusk
with Guacamole Sauce

Roger, who loves hot, spicy foods, features Cajun-style fried fish on the menu of the Park Plaza restaurant he manages. The fish is delicious with a tartar sauce, or with this colorful avocado guacamole sauce. I've suggested cusk because it's a good-tasting, underutilized fish, but you could substitute haddock, cod, wolffish—or any medium-firm to firm-textured white-fleshed fish.

    2 pounds cusk fillets, cut into pieces 1 inch thick
    Buttermilk, for dipping
    Hot pepper sauce
    1 tablespoon Cajun fish seasoning, such as Paul
        Prudhomme's Louisiana Seafood Magic®
    1/3 cup olive oil
    1 cup chopped onions
    1–2 teaspoons chopped garlic
    3 tablespoons chopped green pepper

1–1⅓ pounds avocados, peeled
⅓ cup freshly squeezed lime juice
1 tomato, peeled, seeded and chopped
Salt
¼ teaspoon ground cumin
Vegetable shortening
Flour Mix for Fried Fish

Place the fish in a large bowl, cover with buttermilk, and toss with about 3 dashes of hot pepper sauce and the Cajun seasoning. Let the fish marinate while you make the guacamole sauce.

Heat the olive oil in a large frying pan. Stir in the onions, garlic, and green pepper. Cook over medium heat, stirring frequently, for about 5 minutes, or until the onions are wilted and the pepper is slightly cooked. Place the mixture, including the olive oil, in a food processor and pulse the machine on and off for about 30 seconds.

Add the avocados and the lime juice. Process the mixture until the vegetables are incorporated into the avocado mixture but still have some texture, about 30 seconds. Add the tomatoes, and pulse on and off for a few seconds. Taste the guacamole and season with salt and cumin. Set aside.

Heat the vegetable shortening in a deep, heavy pan until it reaches 350 degrees. The amount of shortening varies depending upon the size of the pot. The fat should be deep enough to cover the fish by about 1 inch.

Toss the cusk in the flour mixture and shake to remove any excess flour. Fry the cusk in the heated fat, a few pieces at a time, about 2½ minutes for each 1-inch-thick piece.

Drain the fish on paper bags. Place the guacamole sauce in a bowl in the center of a large platter, and surround with the fried fish. Serve immediately. (Serves 4)

VARIATIONS:
For a lighter sauce, add ¼ cup mayonnaise to the sauce.
Fried Shrimp with Guacamole Sauce. Substitute shrimp for the cusk, and proceed as above. The shrimp will cook through in about 1 to 1½ minutes, depending upon their size.

Flounder

Flounder Stuffed with Vegetables

The flavors of the carrots and sweet marjoram set off the delicate taste of the flounder. The amount of fish juices exuded by the flounder varies depending upon the type of flatfish. If you lack sufficient juices to make a sauce, omit the last step and serve the fish in the baking pan, spooning over any liquid found in the bottom of the pan.

> 3 tablespoons butter
> 1/2 pound (about 1 1/3 cups) carrots, peeled and finely chopped
> 1 clove garlic, minced
> 1/2 cup chopped scallions (about 6), white parts only
> 1 tablespoon chopped basil
> 2 1/2 tablespoons chopped sweet marjoram
> 2 pounds flounder fillets
> 4 tablespoons heavy cream
> Salt
> Freshly ground black pepper

Heat the butter in a large frying pan and sauté the carrots, garlic, and scallions for about 5 minutes, stirring frequently. The carrots should be barely cooked through. Stir in the basil and 2 tablespoons of the sweet marjoram. Cook for 1 minute longer.

Place the flounder fillets in a row along the counter and equally distribute the filling, covering only half of each fillet. Top with 3/4 to 1 tablespoon cream for each fillet, depending upon how many you have. Season the mixture with salt and pepper. Fold over the remaining halves of the fillets and gently lift them into a buttered baking dish large enough to hold them without crowding. Cover the fish with a buttered piece of foil and place in a preheated 450-degree oven for about 12 to 15 minutes, depending upon the thickness of the flounder.

Remove the fish fillets to a heated platter. Pour the fish juices into a saucepan and reduce them until the sauce is the consistency you wish. Pour it over the fish. Sprinkle with the remaining sweet marjoram. (Serves 4 to 6)

Flounder or Sole Stuffed with Salmon

This is an attractive main course that can be prepared in minutes.

4 tablespoons butter
1/2 cup chopped onions
1 teaspoon chopped garlic
4 ounces chopped raw salmon
1 tablespoon chopped parsley (optional)
2 pounds flounder or sole fillets

Preheat the oven to 425 degrees. Heat the butter in a frying pan, stir in the onions and garlic, and sauté over medium heat for 5 minutes, stirring occasionally. Do not let the mixture brown. Cool it slightly, then stir in the salmon and parsley.

Assemble the fish fillets on the counter and cover half of each fillet with the salmon mixture. Fold over the other half of the fillet to enclose the stuffing.

Place the fillets in a buttered baking dish, and bake for 12 to 15 minutes, or until the fish is cooked through.

Serve immediately, or if you wish, place the fish juices in a pan and boil until they have reduced and thickened to form a sauce. Spoon over the fish and serve. (Serves 4)

VARIATION: *Flounder or Sole Stuffed with Smoked Salmon.* Substitute 3 ounces smoked salmon for the fresh salmon and add 1 tablespoon of chives along with the parsley. Proceed as above, but do not reduce the pan juices or the sauce will be too salty.

Broiled Flounder with Olive Butter

The olive butter perks up the taste of the flounder. This recipe makes enough butter for two meals. Refrigerate the extra butter if you are going to use it within a couple of weeks, or freeze it for future use.

> 1/2 cup butter, softened
> 1/4 cup chopped cocktail olives
> 1/4 teaspoon dry mustard
> 2 pounds flounder fillets

Mix the butter, olives, and mustard together until combined. Set the mixture aside.

Broil the fillets, watching carefully so they don't overcook. When the fillets are cooked through, spread a tablespoon of the olive butter on each one and place back under the broiler for a moment until the butter melts. Serve immediately. (Serves 4)

NOTE: The best way to store the leftover butter is to place it on plastic wrap or foil, form into the shape of a log, wrap it up, and store in the refrigerator or freezer.

VARIATION: *Baked Flounder with Ham and Olive Butter.* Place a thin slice of ham on each flounder fillet, and top with a spoonful of olive butter. Roll up the fish and bake in a preheated 350-degree oven for about 15 minutes or until cooked through. Baste with the pan juices before serving.

See *Sautéed Sole or Flounder* (in the Index).

See also sole listings in the Index.

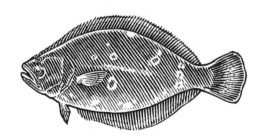

Haddock

Haddock in a Fresh Tomato Sauce

This preparation is good with practically any filleted fish, although white-fleshed fish has a more subtle taste. You could use flounder or sole, but adjust the cooking time depending upon the thickness of the fillets. Remember that tomatoes become more acidic and bitter the longer they cook, so if you want to retain the fresh tomato flavor, cook the sauce only for the length of time suggested.

6 tablespoons olive oil
2/3 cup chopped onions
2 teaspoons minced garlic
9 medium tomatoes, peeled, seeded, and coarsely chopped
3 tablespoons chopped basil
Flour, for dredging
2 pounds haddock, scrod, cusk, or pollock fillets, cut into
    serving pieces
3 tablespoons Parmesan cheese
2/3 cup grated Monterey Jack or mozzarella cheese

Preheat the oven to 375 degrees. Heat 3 tablespoons of the olive oil in a large casserole, and add the onions. Cook for 2 minutes, stirring frequently, or until the onions wilt slightly. Stir in the garlic, and cook 1 minute longer. Add the tomatoes, and cook over medium-high heat for about 10 minutes, stirring frequently. The sauce will retain a slightly chunky texture. Stir in the basil and cook 1 minute longer.

Meanwhile, flour the fish, and shake it to remove any excess. Heat the remaining olive oil in a large frying pan, and sauté the fish for 1 minute on each side, or until barely browned but not cooked through.

Place the fish in an oiled ovenproof dish and top with the tomato sauce. Sprinkle first with the Parmesan cheese, then with the Monterey Jack cheese. Bake for about 10 minutes, or until the fish is cooked through and the cheese is melted. (Serves 4) For a meal-in-one variation, sauté 2 medium sliced zucchini in olive oil until golden, and arrange in a ring around the fish in the baking dish. Top with some of the tomato sauce and proceed as above.

See *Broiled Haddock* (in the Index).

Halibut

Halibut with Asparagus

This dish works equally well with any firm, white-fleshed fish. The eggs taste best if they are boiled just before you cook the asparagus. Shell the eggs and keep them in a pot of warm water.

1¼ pounds fresh asparagus, trimmed
4 tablespoons butter
1 tablespoon vegetable oil
Flour, for dredging
2 pounds halibut steaks, about 1 inch thick
⅓ cup coarsely chopped roasted cashews
2 hard-boiled eggs

Blanch the asparagus in a large pot of boiling water until cooked through but not limp. Using two slotted spoons, remove the asparagus to a towel-covered cake rack to drain.

Heat 2 tablespoons of the butter and the oil together in a large pot. Flour the halibut steaks, shake them to remove the excess, and sauté in the butter until cooked through, turning them once. The time will vary depending upon their thickness. Steaks 1 inch thick will take about 4 minutes each side.

Heat the remaining butter in a clean pan and sauté the nuts 2 to 3 minutes, or long enough to heat them through without burning.

Meanwhile, using a fork, mash the eggs.

Arrange the halibut steaks on a large platter in a spokelike pattern separated by the asparagus spears. Sprinkle some of the mashed eggs over the asparagus, and mound the rest in the center of the platter.

Pour the nuts and butter over the fish, and serve immediately. (Serves 4)

VARIATIONS: Brown the butter before adding the nuts and garnish the eggs with caviar.

Halibut with Broccoli. Substitute blanched broccoli flowerets for the asparagus, and omit the eggs. Just before serving, pour the nuts and butter over the broccoli and halibut.

See *Grilled Halibut* (in the Index).

Halibut with Watercress Sauce

This recipe makes a small quantity of sauce designed to complement rather than smother the halibut. Serve the sauce spooned alongside each serving of fish. During the summer, grill the halibut and substitute fish stock for the pan juices.

1 small onion, chopped
2/3 cup dry white wine
2 pounds halibut steaks, about 1 inch thick
1 tablespoon butter
1/2 cup heavy cream
1/2 cup chopped watercress
1/2–1 teaspoon Dijon mustard
Salt

Preheat the oven to 450 degrees. Place the onions in an enameled, stainless steel, or earthenware baking pan, and pour in the wine. Top with the halibut steaks. Dot them with butter.

Bake the fish for 15 to 20 minutes, or until barely cooked through.

Remove the fish to a heated platter and drape with aluminum foil while you make the sauce.

Pour the pan juices into an enameled or stainless steel saucepan, add the heavy cream, and boil to reduce slightly. Add the watercress, and cook for about 1 minute.

Purée the sauce in a food processor. Taste and add mustard and salt if necessary. Divide the halibut steaks into portions and serve with the sauce. (Serves 4)

Mackerel

Mackerel or Tuna Salad Niçoise

This is a good way to use up leftover fish. It's particularly flavorful with dark-fleshed varieties such as mackerel or tuna, which is the fish used in this traditional salad from the South of France. There's just enough dressing to coat the salad ingredients so that the focus is on the fish and vegetables, not the dressing.

SALAD
3/4–1 pound leftover skinned and boned cooked mackerel, flaked
6–8 canned anchovy fillets (about 1 small can)
4 red peppers, seeded and sliced into rings
4 green peppers, seeded and sliced into rings
5 ripe tomatoes, quartered
1/2 cup pitted black olives, drained
1/2 cup pitted green olives, drained
1 medium onion, chopped
3 hard-boiled eggs, quartered
3 ribs celery, stringed and chopped
4 cups sliced cooked baby potatoes with skins
1 cup cooked green beans

Arrange the mackerel, anchovies, peppers, tomatoes, olives, onions, eggs, celery, potatoes, and beans in a large bowl.

DRESSING
2 teaspoons Dijon mustard
3 tablespoons wine vinegar
5 tablespoons olive oil
2 tablespoons minced fresh basil
1 teaspoon minced fresh tarragon
1/2 teaspoon minced fresh thyme
Salt
Freshly ground black pepper

Mix together the mustard, vinegar, salt, olive oil, and herbs. Taste the mixture and season it with salt and pepper. Just before serving gently toss the salad ingredients with the dressing. (Serves 4 to 6)

Grilled Mackerel
with Garlic Mayonnaise

The mackerel tastes particularly flavorful if it is cooked in a grill that both grills and smokes the fish. Should you wish to serve the fish plain, use the mayonnaise as the base for a homemade potato salad to accompany it.

    4 cloves garlic, peeled and minced
    2 tablespoons lemon juice
    1 teaspoon salt
    3 egg yolks
    1/2 cup plus 1 tablespoon olive oil
    1/2 cup vegetable oil
    4 11/4-pound mackerel, cleaned
    1 lemon, sliced

Place the garlic, lemon juice, salt, and egg yolks in a blender or food processor. Whirl until the garlic is incorporated into the mixture. Either turn the blender to high or start the food processor, and slowly add the olive and vegetable oils. (If you add it too quickly, the mayonnaise doesn't thicken properly.) Place the mayonnaise in a dish, cover with plastic wrap, and refrigerate it for at least 2 hours before serving to allow the flavors a chance to blend.

   You can serve the mackerel either at room temperature or hot from the grill. Either way, oil the fish with the remaining 1 tablespoon olive oil and stuff the cavities with the lemon slices. Grill the mackerel, following the directions for basic Grilling (see Index). (Serves 4)

VARIATION: Add 1/4 cup minced basil or mixed tarragon, chervil, parsley, and basil before you store the mayonnaise in the refrigerator.

Marinated Mackerel

This recipe should be made at least one day ahead of time for maximum flavor. The fish will keep for at least four days in the refrigerator if it is immersed in the marinade in a tightly covered dish.

    Flour, for dredging
    2 pounds mackerel fillets
    Oil, for frying
    3/4 cup wine vinegar
    1 1/4 cups olive oil
    2 tablespoons Dijon mustard
    3 tablespoons minced chives
    2 tablespoons chopped basil
    2 onions, sliced

Flour each fillet and shake to remove any excess flour. Pour oil into a large frying pan until it is 1/4 inch deep. Heat the oil until almost smoking. Fry the mackerel until cooked through and lightly browned, turning once. Remove the fish from the oil and set aside.

Mix together the vinegar, olive oil, mustard, chives, and basil until thoroughly combined.

Arrange the fish and onions in a large deep dish (you will probably have 2 layers) and top with the marinade. If you have more than 1 layer, make sure that some of the marinade covers all of the fish.

Press down slightly to submerge the fish in the marinade. Cover the dish with plastic wrap and place in the refrigerator at least overnight.

The oil may separate slightly in storage, so stir the marinade before serving the fish. (Serves 4 to 6)

VARIATION: *Mackerel with Red Peppers and Onions.* Add 2 sliced red peppers along with the onions, and 2 tablespoons chopped black olives to the marinade. Proceed as above.

Monkfish

Monkfish, Bean, and Pepper Salad

This is a good all-purpose salad. You can substitute any firm-fleshed fish for the monkfish, and broccoli or cauliflower—or a combination of both—for the beans. If you serve the salad dressing on the side, any leftovers can be reassembled for another meal. Cook the monkfish any way you wish: steaming, baking, or grilling all work well.

1/2 pound green beans, trimmed
1 yellow or red pepper, seeded and diced
6 scallions (white parts only), thinly sliced
1 1/2 pounds cooked monkfish, cut in 1/2-inch slices
8–10 ripe cherry tomatoes
4 hard-boiled eggs, quartered (optional)

SALAD DRESSING
1 clove garlic, halved
3/4 teaspoon dry mustard
Salt
Freshly ground black pepper
1/3 cup rice wine or cider vinegar
Scant 1/2 cup vegetable oil
1 teaspoon Dijon mustard
1/4 to 1/3 cup chopped sweet marjoram, or a combination
    of sweet marjoram, parsley, and summer savory

Blanch the beans in a pot of boiling water for about 4 minutes. Plunge into cold water to stop the cooking process, and drain them. Toss with the pepper and scallions.

Assemble the salad. Mound the monkfish in the center of a platter, and surround with the bean mixture. Arrange the cherry tomatoes and eggs on the outside.

Make the dressing. Steep the garlic, mustard, salt, and black pepper in the vinegar for a few minutes. Just before serving, remove the garlic. Stir in the oil, Dijon mustard, and herbs. Either pour the dressing over the salad, or serve in a bowl alongside. (Serves 4)

Monkfish Baked with Herbs and Mustard

This is a good choice for evenings when you're too tired to cook anything elaborate. Dijon mustard works well, as do any of the flavored gourmet mustards put out by the specialty producers. The herbs will darken while cooking. If you prefer, discard them before serving the fish.

2 pounds monkfish fillets
1/3 cup chopped basil or a mixture of basil and parsley
2 tablespoons Dijon or spicy mustard
Freshly ground black pepper
4 slices raw bacon

Place the monkfish on the counter and make parallel cuts across the fillets about 1/2 inch deep and 11/2 inches apart. Divide up the herbs and stuff the cuts. Spread the mustard on the fillets, sprinkle with black pepper, and top with the bacon.

Place the fillets in an ovenproof dish and bake in a preheated 425-degree oven for 10 to 15 minutes, depending upon the thickness of the fillets. Serve in slices. (Serves 4)

VARIATION: Sauté 1/2 pound chopped mushrooms and 1/4 cup chopped onions in 2 to 3 tablespoons butter and stuff the fillets with this mixture rather than the herbs. You can also add 1/4 cup grated Parmesan cheese to the mixture.

Pollock

Pollock with Corn, Zucchini, and Peppers

You can substitute any firm, white-fleshed fish for the pollock. This dish tastes best made with fresh vegetables. It is a meal-in-one.

    7 tablespoons vegetable oil, or a mixture of olive and
        vegetable oil
    2 onions, chopped
    3 cloves garlic, minced
    2 Italian frying peppers, coarsely chopped, or 1 large red
        bell pepper, chopped
    4 cups corn kernels (about 6 ears corn)
    1 small zucchini, quartered lengthwise and cut into ¾-inch
        pieces
    2 ripe tomatoes, peeled, seeded, and coarsely chopped
    ⅓ cup chopped basil
    2 pounds pollock fillets
    Cumin
    Salt
    Freshly ground black pepper
    1 tablespoon chopped chives

Heat 3 tablespoons of the oil in a large frying pan and sauté the onions and garlic for about 5 minutes. Add the peppers, corn, and zucchini, and cook another 3 minutes, stirring frequently. Stir in the tomatoes and basil. Remove the pan from the heat.

  Meanwhile, sprinkle the pollock fillets with a light dusting of cumin. Heat the remaining oil in another frying pan. Fry the fillets in the oil until they are cooked through, turning once. This will take 5 to 8 minutes, depending upon the thickness of the fish.

With a slotted spoon, remove the fillets and arrange them in the center of a platter. Reheat the corn mixture if necessary, taste and season with salt and pepper, and pour the mixture around the fish. Sprinkle the fish with the chives. (Serves 4 to 6)

VARIATION: Add 3 tablespoons soft goat cheese and 1 tablespoon chopped chives to the vegetables. Cook for 1 minute to melt the cheese, and spoon around the fish.

Pollock. See *Fried Pollock* (in the Index).

Pollock may be substituted for cod or haddock.

Salmon

Salmon Fillets Stuffed with Scallop Mousse

This is an exceptionally easy yet splashy main course. The mint and chives set off the flavor of the salmon and scallops. If you wish, omit the butter-lime-juice-chive sauce.

> 1/2 pound scallops
> 2 egg whites
> 1/2 teaspoon salt
> 2 tablespoons heavy cream
> 1/4 teaspoon dry mustard
> 1 tablespoon minced fresh mint leaves
> 2 teaspoons chopped chives plus 2 tablespoons
> 2 pounds salmon fillets, cut 1/4 inch thick
> 5 tablespoons butter
> 1 tablespoon freshly squeezed lime juice

Preheat the oven to 425 degrees. Purée the scallops, egg whites, salt, cream, and mustard in a food processor. Stir in the mint leaves and 2 teaspoons of the chives. The mixture will have a soft consistency.

Lay the salmon fillets in a row on the counter, and spread them with the scallop mixture. Roll them up. (If any of the stuffing oozes out, gently push it back into place.) Put the fillets in a buttered baking dish, dot with 1 tablespoon of the butter, and bake for about 15 minutes, or until the fish and stuffing are cooked through.

While the fillets are cooking, melt the remaining butter. Stir in the lime juice and chives. Pour the butter sauce over the fish just before serving. (Serves 4)

Chilled Salmon and Cucumber Soup

Try this soup as a main course on a steamy summer evening.

    1 1/4-pound salmon fillet
    1 medium onion, diced
    3 cups Fish Stock or clam stock
    3 cucumbers, peeled, seeded, and diced
    1 1/2–2 tablespoons chopped fresh dill leaves
    2 1/2 cups plain yogurt
    Salt
    Freshly ground black pepper

Steam the salmon until just cooked through. Let cool, then refrigerate.

Mix the onions with the Fish Stock and cucumbers. Place the mixture in a saucepan and cook over low heat until the cucumbers are tender but not mushy, about 5 minutes. Pulse in a food processor or blender with the fresh dill and yogurt just until combined. Season with salt and pepper to taste. Chill.

Just before serving, flake the salmon and add the pieces to the soup. Garnish with additional chopped cucumbers and dill if you wish. (Serves 4 to 6)

Salmon with a Sweet and Sour Coriander Sauce

The coriander and grapefruit flavors balance the rich taste of the salmon.

2 pounds salmon steaks
3 tablespoons butter
1/3 cup chopped onions
2 tablespoons chopped coriander
2 tablespoons white wine vinegar
1/3 cup freshly squeezed grapefruit juice
1/4 teaspoon Dijon mustard
1/8–1/4 teaspoon cumin
Coriander leaves (optional)
Peeled grapefruit slices (optional)

Preheat the broiler. Broil the salmon for about 4 to 5 minutes on each side, depending upon the thickness. Remove the salmon from the broiler and let it sit while you finish the sauce.

While the salmon is broiling, make the coriander sauce. Heat the butter in a large enameled or stainless steel frying pan and stew the onions for 5 minutes in the butter, stirring frequently. Add the coriander and cook for 1 minute, stirring constantly. Add the vinegar, turn up the heat, and cook rapidly for about 2 minutes, stirring constantly, until the vinegar practically evaporates. Remove from the heat, stir in the grapefruit juice, mustard, and cumin. Lower heat and cook for 1 minute longer, stirring constantly, or until the sauce is the thickness you wish.

Place the sauce on a platter and top with the salmon steaks. Garnish with coriander leaves and grapefruit slices. (Serves 4)

VARIATION: *Swordfish with Coriander and Red Pepper Sauce.* Substitute swordfish steaks for the salmon. Follow the recipe above, but substitute 1/4 teaspoon ground fenugreek for the cumin, and add 2–3 tablespoons chopped roasted red peppers just before serving. (Fenugreek is an Indian spice found in gourmet or ethnic food shops.)

Broiled Coho Salmon
with a Chive Butter Sauce

Many of our customers like Coho salmon butterflied and broiled. (Any fishmonger should be able to butterfly the salmon and remove their heads.) This tart sauce, inspired by the French beurre blanc sauce—but with much less fat—perks up the flavor of the rather bland Coho salmon. This recipe calls for only a tablespoon of sauce per serving so that the salmon flavor is not overwhelmed by the sauce. If you prefer more sauce with your fish, whisk in 4 tablespoons additional butter and add additional herbs to taste.

> 4 Coho salmon (about 4 pounds), butterflied or filleted
> 1 tablespoon vegetable oil
> 1/4 cup white wine vinegar
> 1/4 cup dry white wine
> 3 tablespoons minced scallions (white parts only), onions, or shallots
> 1/2 cup butter, chilled and cut into pieces
> 1 tablespoon minced chives
> 1 teaspoon minced sweet marjoram or basil
> 1 teaspoon grated orange rind (optional)
> Salt
> Dash cayenne pepper

Coat the butterflied salmon pieces with oil and broil or grill them until they are cooked through. The salmon pieces will cook more rapidly than you might expect, so watch them carefully. If the pieces cook through before the sauce is completed, place them on a heated platter.

While the salmon is cooking, make the butter sauce. Place the vinegar, white wine, and scallions in an enameled or stainless steel saucepan. Bring the liquid to a boil and slowly boil the mixture until the liquid is reduced to 1 tablespoon. This will take 2 to 3 minutes. Turn the heat to low and slowly whisk in the butter, piece by piece. The sauce will thicken and turn golden.

Add the chives, sweet marjoram, and orange rind. Taste and season with the salt and cayenne pepper.

Put a spoonful of sauce on each piece of salmon and serve immediately. (Serves 4)

See *Poached Salmon* (in Index).

Stuffed Coho Salmon

Ask your fishmonger to split, gut, and bone the salmon for you. To string the celery, make a cut into the end of the stalk, then pull out and downward. The strings will separate from the celery stalk in the process.

> 2 small Coho salmon (about 2 pounds), about 10 inches long, split, gutted, and boned
> Salt
> Freshly ground pepper
> 2 tablespoons butter
> 1/3 cup chopped onions
> 2 tablespoons chopped green pepper
> 1/3 cup chopped celery, with strings removed
> 1 cup chopped mushrooms
> 1 1/3 cup fresh bread crumbs, made from densely textured bread
> 2 tablespoons chopped parsley
> Dash cayenne pepper
> Vegetable oil

Preheat the oven to 350 degrees. Wash and dry the salmon, then salt and pepper the body cavities. Heat the butter in a large frying pan, and sauté the onions, green pepper, and celery for about 5 minutes, stirring frequently. Stir in the mushrooms, and sauté about 3 minutes longer. Stir in the bread crumbs, parsley, cayenne pepper. Taste the stuffing and season with salt and pepper if necessary.

Oil a baking pan. Oil the exterior of the fish. Loosely stuff the fish with the bread-crumb mixture, and fasten the cavities shut with toothpicks. Bake for about 15 to 20 minutes, or until the salmon seems firm when you press down upon it. Cut into serving pieces. (Serves 4)

Scrod

Scrod Stuffed with Shrimp and Mushrooms

This is the favorite lunchtime special at the restaurants Roger manages. Try to buy scrod tail fillets because they're easier to roll. If that's not possible, you can always butterfly the scrod to the right thickness; aim for fish 3/4 inch thick. The tiny, delicately flavored Maine shrimp are in season during the winter months. If you can't find them, substitute chopped raw shrimp or cooked tiny Norwegian shrimp.

    6 tablespoons butter
    4 tablespoons minced onions
    2 teaspoons chopped garlic
    4 ounces chopped mushrooms (1/4 pound)
    4 tablespoons dry sherry
    8 ounces peeled Maine shrimp or chopped gulf shrimp
    2 pounds scrod fillets, in 4 pieces
    About 1/2 cup milk
    1/2–3/4 cup Cracker Crumb Mixture

Preheat the oven to 450 degrees. Melt 4 tablespoons of the butter in an enameled or stainless steel frying pan. Slowly cook the onions and garlic for 3 to 4 minutes. Do not let them brown.

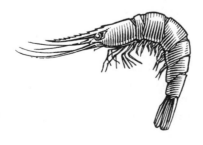

Add the mushrooms and cook for about 3 minutes, or until wilted, stirring frequently. Pour in the sherry, turn the heat to high, and cook, stirring constantly, until the sherry has been absorbed by the vegetables. Stir in the shrimp and cook, stirring constantly, for about 1 minute—just long enough to firm them slightly; the shrimp should not cook through. Set the mixture aside to cool slightly.

Dip the fish pieces into the milk, and then into the cracker crumbs. Lay the fish out on the counter and center a quarter of the shrimp mixture on each piece. Fold over the ends of each piece until they meet, just covering the shrimp mixture.

Place the fish pieces, seam side down, into a buttered baking dish. The size of the dish is important—you want the fish to be closely packed but not crowded. Pat cracker crumbs over the top of each serving, pressing down slightly so the crumbs will adhere. Dot the fish with the remaining 2 tablespoons butter.

Bake for 20 to 25 minutes, or until the crumbs are browned and the fish is cooked through. Do not overcook. The fish may exude some juices; spoon them over the top before serving. (Serves 4)

Savory Scrod

This recipe is an excellent choice for any thick, white-fleshed fish fillets. It is particularly good with fresh summer vegetables, although it also works well with winter tomatoes—just increase the amount of tomatoes to compensate for the lack of juice, and add dried oregano or basil for flavor.

1/2 cup olive oil
6 cups sliced onions (about 2 large onions)
2 cloves garlic, minced
1 green pepper, seeded and sliced
2 pounds tomatoes (about 4 large tomatoes), peeled, seeded, and chopped
1/4 pound feta cheese, finely chopped
2 pounds scrod fillets, cut into serving pieces
Flour, for dredging
3 tablespoons freshly grated Parmesan cheese

Preheat the oven to 400 degrees. Heat 1/4 cup of the olive oil in a large frying pan and sauté the onions and garlic slowly for about 10 minutes, stirring frequently. Add the green pepper and cook, stirring constantly, for about 2 minutes. Stir in the tomatoes and cook for about 5 minutes, stirring frequently. Stir in the feta cheese and cook for about 2 minutes, stirring frequently. Set the sauce aside, and clean out the pan.

Heat the remaining olive oil in the pan. Dip the fish fillets in the flour, shake off any excess, and brown in the oil, about 1 minute on each side. (The fish will finish cooking in the oven.)

Select a baking pan into which the fish will fit snugly, and spread some of the sauce on the bottom of the pan. Top with the fish fillets. Sprinkle the Parmesan cheese over the fish, and top with the remaining sauce.

Bake for about 15 to 20 minutes, or until the fish is cooked through. Baste the fish with the sauce occasionally. Serve with rice. (Serves 4 to 6)

VARIATION: Substitute halibut or cusk fillets for the scrod, and add 1 sliced zucchini and 1 cup sliced mushrooms along with the pepper.

Scrod in a Tarragon Cream Sauce

The juices exuded by the scrod as it bakes are used in the sauce.

    2 pounds scrod
    1/2 cup heavy cream
    1 1/2 teaspoons chopped fresh tarragon *or* 1/2 teaspoon
        dried tarragon
    1 teaspoon French mustard made with coarsely ground
        mustard seeds
    Freshly ground black pepper
    1 tablespoon grated Parmesan or Romano cheese

Preheat the oven to 425 degrees. Place the scrod in a buttered baking dish and bake for about 15 minutes or until it is barely cooked through. Pour the fish juices into a saucepan. Keep the fish warm while you make the sauce.

Add the heavy cream to the fish juices, raise the heat, and

gently boil the mixture, stirring frequently, until it thickens. Add the tarragon, mustard, pepper, and cheese, and cook for about 2 minutes longer.

Pour the sauce over the fish and serve immediately. (Serves 4)

Scrod Baked with Mayonnaise and Crumbs

This easily prepared dish is a favorite of our employees at staff lunches. You don't taste the mayonnaise as such—it merely keeps the fish moist and holds the crumb topping. Homemade mayonnaise is best, but if you're using a commercial variety, make sure it doesn't contain sugar, which would mask the taste of the fish. Substitute any white fish fillets for the scrod.

> 2 pounds scrod fillets, about 1 inch thick
> 1/4 cup Easy Blender Mayonnaise
> 1/3 cup Cracker Crumb Mixture

Preheat the oven to 425 degrees. Place the fillets in a baking dish just large enough to hold them. Thinly spread with mayonnaise and top them with the crumb mixture.

Bake the fillets for about 12 to 15 minutes, or until they are cooked through. (Serves 4)

VARIATIONS:

Scrod Baked with Herb Cheese and Crumbs. Combine the mayonnaise with 2–3 tablespoons commercially prepared herb-garlic cheese such as Boursin, and proceed as above.

Scrod Baked with Cheese and Crumbs. Mix 2 tablespoons freshly grated Parmesan cheese into the mayonnaise and proceed as above.

Scrod Baked with Tahini and Crumbs. Mix 1–2 tablespoons tahini (sesame seed paste) into the mayonnaise and proceed as above.

See *Baked Scrod* (in the Index).

Shad Roe

Shad Roe with Bacon

This is an excellent spring brunch or light supper dish.

8 slices lean bacon
2 pair shad roe, about 1 1/4 pounds
Freshly ground black pepper
Flour, for dredging
2 lemons, quartered

Cook the bacon in a heavy skillet until it is crisp, and set aside.

Sprinkle the roe with pepper, dip in flour, and dust off any excess. Sauté the roe in the bacon fat left in the pan, for 5 minutes each side. Cover with a steamer lid while cooking.

Remove the roe to a platter, and divide along the connecting membrane. Top with bacon slices, and serve surrounded by lemon wedges. (Serves 2 to 4)

VARIATION: *Shad Roe with Bacon, Mushrooms, and Tomatoes.* Proceed as above. Keep the roe warm while you sauté thickly sliced mushrooms and halved tomatoes in the remaining bacon fat. Serve alongside the roe.

Sautéed Shad Roe with Lemon and Chives

4–6 tablespoons butter
2 pair shad roe, about 1 1/4 pounds
Flour, for dredging
1/4 cup freshly squeezed lemon juice (about 1 lemon)
2 tablespoons minced chives

In a heavy frying pan, heat the butter. Dip the roe in flour, dust off any excess, and place in the pan. Cover with the lid of a steamer, and gently sauté for about 5 minutes. Turn the roe, and sauté for another 5 minutes. Do not overcook.

Remove the roe to a serving platter, and divide each pair by cutting along the connecting membrane. Stir the lemon juice into the pan juices, then add the chives and cook for about 15 seconds. Pour the sauce over the roe and serve immediately. (Serves 2 to 4)

Sole

Sole Stuffed with Spinach and Cheese

This attractive yet easy to prepare dish was developed by our son Marc to serve at the Legal Sea Foods restaurants he manages.

2 tablespoons minced scallions (white parts only)
1 cup coarsely chopped stemmed spinach
2 tablespoons minced parsley
1 cup grated Monterey Jack cheese
2 pounds gray sole fillets (about 4 pieces)
Salt (optional)
8 tablespoons Cracker Crumb Mixture
Milk
2 tablespoons butter

Preheat the oven to 350 degrees. Mix together the scallions, spinach, parsley, and 3/4 cup of the cheese. Set the mixture aside.

Spread the fish fillets out on the counter. Sprinkle with salt if you wish, and then with half of the cracker crumbs (about 1 tablespoon per fillet). Top each fillet with one quarter of the spinach mixture.

Fold each fillet into thirds, forming packets. Dip the fish packets into milk and then sprinkle with the remaining crumbs. Place them in a buttered baking dish. Sprinkle with the remaining cheese, and dot each fish packet with 1/2 tablespoon butter.

Bake the fish for about 15 minutes, or until cooked through.

Be sure to remove the fish packets from the oven the moment they are done, because overcooking destroys the moist texture of the fish. If you wish, run the fish under the broiler to brown the cheese. Serve immediately. (Serves 4)

Easy Baked Sole

This recipe is for days when you have about one minute to fix dinner.

    5 tablespoons butter
    2 cloves garlic, minced
    1 tomato, peeled, seeded, and chopped
    2 tablespoons grated Parmesan cheese
    2 tablespoons chopped basil, *or* 1 tablespoon chopped
        sweet marjoram or parsley
    2 pounds sole fillets

Preheat the oven to 375 degrees. Heat 4 tablespoons of the butter in a small saucepan until it is bubbling. Add the garlic and tomatoes and cook for 30 seconds, stirring. Turn off the heat and stir in the cheese and basil.

Lay the fish out on the counter and spread half of each fillet with the butter-cheese mixture. Fold over the other half of the fillet, as if you were folding a piece of paper. A little butter may leak out of the sides of the fish, but that doesn't matter.

Place the fillets in a buttered baking dish, and dot with the remaining butter. Bake for about 15 minutes. If you wish, before serving reduce the pan juices and pour over the fish. (Serves 4)

Breaded Sole with Herbs

The bread-crumb coating keeps the sole moist and tender. For best results use fine dry bread crumbs from a good-quality bread. An egg bread, such as challah, is an excellent choice. Dried herbes de Provence are stocked by many supermarkets.

    1 1/3 cups fine dry bread crumbs
    1 teaspoon dried herbes de Provence
    1/2 teaspoon salt
    2 eggs
    1/4 cup whipping cream
    2 pounds sole or flounder fillets
    1/2 cup butter

Combine the bread crumbs, herbs, and salt in a large shallow bowl and place on the counter.

Beat together the eggs and cream, add the fish fillets, and stir to coat. Let the fillets sit in the cream mixture for 5 minutes, then dip them in the seasoned bread crumbs. Each fillet should be thoroughly coated with a layer of crumbs.

Heat 5 tablespoons of the butter in a large frying pan, add half the fillets, and cook them about 2 minutes on each side. Regulate the heat so that the bread-crumb coating browns but doesn't burn. Remove from the heat. Add the rest of the butter and cook the remaining fillets. Do not crowd the pan or the fish will steam slightly and the crumb coating on the fillets will fall off. Serve the fish immediately. (Serves 4)

Sole Stuffed with Crabmeat

This delicately flavored fish dish, made with East Coast crabmeat, is easy to prepare.

    2 tablespoons butter
    2–3 tablespoons scallions, white parts only, chopped
    1 stalk celery, stringed and chopped
    1/2 cup chopped mushrooms
    8 ounces fresh crabmeat

3 tablespoons mayonnaise
1/2 teaspoon dry mustard
Salt
Juice of 1 lemon
2 pounds sole fillets
2 teaspoons butter
Chopped parsley (optional)

Preheat the oven to 375 degrees. Heat the butter in a large frying pan, and stir in the scallions and celery. Cook them for about 2 minutes over medium heat, stirring frequently. Add the mushrooms and cook for 2 to 3 minutes, or until the mushrooms are cooked through and have exuded their juices. Cool the mixture slightly.

Stir the mushroom mixture into the crabmeat. Add the mayonnaise, dry mustard, salt, and about 1 teaspoon of the lemon juice.

Lay the sole out on the counter. Spread the crabmeat mixture over half of each piece of sole, then fold over the other half. You will have the equivalent of a hinged sandwich of sole with crabmeat in the center.

Place the sole in a buttered baking dish and dot with the butter. Pour the remaining lemon juice over each piece. Bake for about 15 to 20 minutes, or until the fish is cooked through. Lightly sprinkle with parsley before serving. (Serves 4)

See the *Flounder* recipes in the Index.

Sole Stuffed with Shrimp

The shrimp stuffing cooks along with the sole in this splashy yet easy to prepare dish. You can vary the flavor of the stuffing by changing the herbs. Parsley gives the most subtle flavor, while sweet marjoram or chervil are good springtime choices.

    1/2 pound cleaned shrimp
    2 eggs, separated
    1/2 teaspoon salt
    5 tablespoons light cream
    1/4 teaspoon dry mustard
    1–2 tablespoons minced parsley, sweet marjoram, or
        chervil
    2 pounds sole or flounder fillets
    1 cup dried bread crumbs
    1 tablespoon butter

Preheat the oven to 425 degrees. Purée the shrimp, 2 egg whites, salt, 2 tablespoons of the cream, and the dry mustard in a food processor. Stir in the herbs. The mixture will have a soft pastelike consistency.

Lay the sole fillets out on the counter, and spread them with the shrimp mixture. Roll them up. Beat the egg yolks with the remaining 3 tablespoons cream, and dip the fillets into this mixture. Coat with the bread crumbs.

Place the fillets in a buttered baking dish and bake for about 15 minutes, or until the fish and stuffing are cooked through. Just before serving, place slivers of butter over each fillet and place them back in the oven to melt the butter. Serve immediately. (Serves 4)

Swordfish

Swordfish with Summer Vegetables

This is an excellent way to prepare thickly sliced fish fillets.

5–6 tablespoons olive oil
Flour, for dredging
2 pounds swordfish fillets, about 1 inch thick
1¼ cups sliced onions
2 cloves garlic, minced
1 green pepper, seeded and thinly sliced
3 medium tomatoes (about 1 pound), peeled, seeded, and
    sliced
¼ pound mushrooms, thinly sliced
1 tablespoon fresh basil, minced
8 black olives, stoned and halved
A dash cayenne pepper
⅓ cup lemon juice
Salt (optional)

Preheat the oven to 350 degrees. Heat 2 tablespoons of the oil in a large frying pan. Lightly flour the swordfish and sauté it for about 2 minutes on each side. The fish should not be cooked through.

Place the fish in a large baking dish, and set it aside. Wipe out the frying pan, add the remaining oil, and sauté the onions, garlic, and green pepper for about 2 minutes, stirring constantly. Add the tomatoes and cook another 5 minutes, stirring frequently. Stir in the mushrooms and basil, and continue cooking until the mushrooms are cooked through, about 4 minutes. Add the olives, cayenne pepper, and lemon juice. Taste the sauce and add salt if necessary.

Pour the sauce over the swordfish and bake for about 10 to 15 minutes, basting frequently, or until the swordfish is cooked through. (Serves 4)

Swordfish Kabobs

These kabobs are perennial favorites at our restaurants. In good
weather grill them outdoors on a barbecue; during the winter
broil them in the oven. If you're using tomatoes ripened in the
garden, select ones that are still firm—otherwise they will fall
apart while cooking.

    1/3 cup freshly squeezed lemon juice
    2/3 cup vegetable oil
    1 teaspoon dried basil or herbes de Provence
    A pinch dry mustard
    Freshly ground black pepper to taste
    1¾ pounds swordfish, cut into chunks 1½–2 inches thick
        (about 24 pieces)
    16 mushroom caps (about ¼ pound)
    4 medium Bermuda onions, quartered
    4 medium tomatoes, quartered
    2 large green peppers, quartered then halved

Place the lemon juice, vegetable oil, herbs, mustard, and black
pepper in the bowl of a food processor. Whirl the ingredients
until combined. Or, whisk them by hand in a large bowl.

Toss together the swordfish chunks and the mushrooms with
the oil mixture, and set aside to marinate for at least one hour.

Preheat the oven to 550 degrees. Assemble the kabobs, allot-
ing two skewers per person. On each skewer place a mushroom
cap, swordfish chunk, onion wedge, tomato quarter, piece of
pepper, swordfish chunk, onion wedge, tomato quarter, piece of
pepper, swordfish chunk, and mushroom cap.

Place the kabobs on a broiling pan, and brush them with the
marinade remaining in the bowl. Broil for about 12 minutes,
turning once, and basting with additional oil if necessary. Serve
immediately. (Serves 4)

VARIATION: *Scallop Kabobs.* Substitute large sea scallops for the
swordfish chunks, and lime juice for the lemon juice if you wish.

Broil only about 10 minutes, checking after 8 minutes, because scallops cook faster than swordfish chunks.

Swordfish with Tomatoes and Mussels

This beautiful company dish should be made with absolutely ripe tomatoes. Cooked this way the swordfish has a tender, moist texture.

- 6 tablespoons olive oil
- 1 cup chopped onions
- 1 teaspoon chopped garlic
- 2 cups peeled, seeded, and chopped ripe tomatoes
- 2 pounds swordfish steaks, about 1 inch thick, cut into serving pieces
- 1/2 pound mussels, cleaned
- 2 tablespoons chopped fresh basil

Heat 3 tablespoons of the olive oil in a large stovetop casserole, and sauté the onions and garlic for about 10 minutes, stirring frequently, or until wilted but not browned. Stir in the tomatoes and cook for 5 minutes.

Meanwhile, heat the remaining oil in a large frying pan and brown the swordfish on both sides. Do not cook it through.

Place the swordfish in the casserole and top with the mussels. Cover casserole and cook slowly for 10 to 15 minutes, or until the swordfish is cooked through and the mussels have opened. Remove the swordfish to a platter, and surround with the mussels. Cover with a towel to keep the fish warm.

Raise the heat and reduce the tomato mixture until the excess liquid evaporates, and it has a saucelike consistency, about 5 minutes. Add the basil and cook for 2 minutes longer. Pour the tomato sauce over the fish. Serve immediately. (Serves 4)

Swordfish with Oysters

This exceptionally easy dish takes but a moment to assemble. The amount of oysters needed depends upon their size.

4 swordfish fillets (about 1¼ pounds), cut about ¼ inch thick
Dijon mustard
12–16 oysters, shucked
Toothpicks
4 tablespoons butter (optional)
1 tablespoon minced chives (optional)

Preheat the oven to 375 degrees. Place the swordfish fillets on the counter and spread them with a thin coating of mustard. Use the mustard sparingly—about ½ teaspoon should be more than sufficient. Arrange 3–4 oysters on each fillet and fold over the sides of the fillet to enclose the oysters. Fasten with toothpicks.

Bake for about 15 minutes, or until cooked through. You can either serve the fish plain or top just before serving with the butter-chive mixture. Heat the butter until bubbling, stir in the chives, and pour over the fish. (Serves 4)

Grilled Swordfish with Orange Sauce

While the swordfish is grilling you have plenty of time to make a glazelike sauce. The vinegar and lemon juice keep it from being too sweet.

2 pounds swordfish steaks, cut 1 inch thick
About ½ cup olive oil or vegetable oil
4 tablespoons butter
½ cup chopped scallions, white parts only
1 tablespoon red wine vinegar
2 tablespoons orange juice concentrate (do not dilute)
2 tablespoons freshly squeezed lemon juice
1 teaspoon Dijon mustard

Marinate the swordfish in the oil for a few minutes before grilling it. Place the fish on the grill and cook for about 5 to 8 minutes per side, testing after 5 minutes to see if the fish is done. The cooking time will vary depending upon the temperature of the coals.

Meanwhile, make the sauce. Heat the butter in an enameled or stainless steel frying pan and sauté the scallions for 3 minutes, or until they are slightly wilted. Stir in the vinegar and cook, stirring frequently, until the vinegar has almost evaporated. Reduce the heat, and add the orange juice concentrate and lemon juice. Stir constantly until the ingredients form a sauce with an almost glazelike consistency. Stir in the mustard, taste the sauce, and add more lemon juice if needed. Spoon the sauce over the fish and serve immediately. (Serves 4)

Broiled Swordfish with Salsa

This Mexican salsa, inspired by the food of the Yucatán, is an excellent foil for the rich taste of the swordfish. Try it with other oily fish such as mackerel or bluefish. Use up the salsa within a day—otherwise it loses its fresh, pleasant flavor.

SALSA
4–5 large tomatoes, peeled, seeded, and chopped
1 cup chopped Bermuda onion
2–3 hot peppers, such as jalapeños, seeded and minced
1/4 cup freshly squeezed orange juice
Juice of 1 lime
2 tablespoons chopped fresh coriander
Salt (optional)
2 pounds swordfish steaks, about 1 inch thick
1/2 cup olive oil
Juice of 1 large lemon
Freshly ground black pepper

Mix together the tomatoes, onions, peppers, orange juice, lime juice, coriander, and salt to taste in a large bowl. Press down slightly on the mixture to extract some of the tomato juices. Cover the bowl with plastic wrap, and set aside for at least 1 hour to allow the flavors a chance to meld.

Preheat the broiler. Marinate the fish in a mixture of about 2/3 oil to 1/3 lemon juice for a few minutes before broiling. Drain the fish, reserving the marinade. Broil the fish for about 5 minutes on each side—or until cooked through, basting occasionally with the reserved marinade. Serve with the salsa and a plate of cornbread. (Serves 4)

VARIATION: Substitute tuna for swordfish and replace coriander with basil.

Tuna

Grilled Tuna with a Cucumber Garnish

The cucumber garnish is inspired by the sweet-sour cucumber salad often served in Denmark and Sweden. The green color is attractive set against the brown of the tuna.

    2 pounds tuna steak, about 1 inch thick
    3 tablespoons vegetable oil
    Juice of 1 lemon
    2 medium cucumbers (about 10 ounces)
    1/2 teaspoon salt
    2 tablespoons sugar
    4 tablespoons cider vinegar

Marinate the tuna in the oil and the lemon juice for about 1 hour before grilling.

Score and thinly slice the cucumbers. Place them in a bowl and toss with the salt. Mix in the sugar and vinegar. Press down upon the cucumbers with a wooden spoon to extract some of the cucumber liquid. Let the cucumbers marinate for at least 30 minutes.

Grill the tuna until just cooked through, turning once; about 8 to 10 minutes, depending upon the heat of the flame.

Cut the tuna into serving pieces. Serve each portion with a garnish of the cucumbers alongside, removed from the marinade with a slotted spoon. (Serves 4)

NOTE: The cucumbers will keep for 4 to 5 days in the refrigerator if stored in the marinade in a covered dish.

Fresh Tuna in a Lemon-Caper Sauce

The lemon juice and capers accentuate the tuna flavor.

2 pounds tuna steaks, about 1 inch thick
Vegetable oil
5 tablespoons butter
2 cloves garlic, minced
3/4 cup chopped onion
1/2 cup freshly squeezed lemon juice
2 tablespoons minced capers

Brush the tuna steaks with oil and broil or grill them until cooked through, about 5 minutes on each side.

Meanwhile, heat the butter in a frying pan and slowly sauté the garlic and onion until softened, about 5 minutes. Stir in the lemon juice and capers, and cook for 1 minute. Spoon the sauce over the tuna and serve immediately. (Serves 4)

VARIATION: *Tuna with Lime Juice.* Omit the capers. Substitute 1/4–1/3 cup freshly squeezed lime juice for the lemon juice and add 1/4 teaspoon good-quality soy sauce and a dash of cayenne pepper.

Wolffish

Wolffish Parmigiana

Wolffish, which is also called ocean catfish, is a fine-flavored white-fleshed fish. You could substitute any white-fleshed fish, such as cod, halibut, haddock, or cusk for the wolffish, and a good-quality commercial tomato sauce for the homemade version.

> 1/2 cup olive oil
> 2 pounds wolffish fillets
> 1 1/2 cups Fresh Tomato Sauce
> 1 large onion, thinly sliced
> 1 green pepper, chopped
> 1 hot pepper, minced (optional)
> 1 clove garlic, minced
> 1 cup sliced mushrooms
> 1 tablespoon chopped basil
> 4 ounces mozzarella cheese, coarsely grated
> 1/2 cup grated Parmesan cheese

Preheat the oven to 400 degrees. Heat the olive oil in a large frying pan, and brown the fish on both sides. Place 1/2 cup of the tomato sauce in the bottom of a baking dish just large enough to hold the fish. Top with the fish.

With the fish removed from the frying pan, and using the same oil, sauté the onions, green pepper, and garlic for 2 minutes, stirring frequently. Stir in the mushrooms and cook rapidly until they have released their juices. Stir in the basil and cook for 30 seconds, then stir in the remaining 1 cup tomato sauce.

Pour the tomato sauce and the vegetables over the fish. Sprinkle with the mozzarella and Parmesan cheeses. Bake for about 15 minutes, or until the fish is cooked through. (Serves 4)

Wolffish in a Mushroom Sauce

You can substitute any thick, white-fleshed fish fillets for the wolffish. This technique of oven steaming fish is useful anytime you want to end up with a quantity of fish juices for a sauce. If you prefer, use half sweet and half hot red peppers for a hotter sauce.

2 pounds wolffish fillets
1 lemon, halved
2 stalks lovage or celery leaves
4 tablespoons butter
1 tablespoon vegetable oil
8 ounces mushrooms, thinly sliced
1 clove garlic, minced
3 tablespoons minced sweet red pepper or a combination
  of sweet and hot peppers
2 tablespoons flour
1/2 cup fish juices
2/3 cup heavy cream
1 tablespoon dry sherry
2 tablespoons chopped parsley
Lemon slices (optional)

Preheat the oven to 425 degrees. Cut a piece of aluminum foil large enough to enclose the fish fillets. Center the fillets on the foil, squeeze the juice of the lemon over them, and top with the lovage or celery leaves. Make an envelope of the foil and place it in a baking dish. Bake the fish for about 12 minutes, or until it is cooked through.

While the fish is cooking, start the mushroom sauce. Heat 2 tablespoons of the butter and the oil together in a frying pan. Add the mushrooms and garlic, and cook, stirring frequently, for about 5 minutes or until the mushrooms have exuded their juices. Stir in the red pepper, raise the heat, and cook, stirring constantly, for 2 minutes. Set the vegetable mixture aside.

Remove the fillets from the oven and place on a heated platter. Pour the fish juices into a measuring cup. You should have about 1/2 cup. (If you don't, add water.) Melt the remaining butter in an enameled or stainless steel pot, and stir in the flour. Cook for 2 minutes over low heat, stirring frequently. Remove from the heat, add the fish juices, and whisk until they are combined with the flour. Return the pot to the stove and cook for 2 minutes over medium heat, stirring frequently.

Stir in the cream and sherry, and cook 1 minute longer to remove the raw taste of the alcohol. Add the parsley. Pour the sauce over the fish, and garnish with lemon slices. Serve immediately. (Serves 4)

Shellfish

People who won't touch fish will eat shellfish at the drop of a hat. We serve almost four thousand pounds of shrimp every week at our restaurants—not to mention the staggering amount of native lobsters, clams, mussels, oysters, scallops, squid, and crabmeat that our customers stash away.

I've had customers ask me why the shellfish we serve tastes so much better than that found in other areas of the country. Our shellfish is fresh, of course, but there's an equally valid reason why our shellfish is so good. New England has large areas of unpolluted waters, such as Cape Cod, that are teeming with the nutrients upon which shellfish feed. The bay scallops that come from the clean waters off Cape Cod, for example, have a sweet, almost sugary, flavor that's unique in the scallop world. Farther south, pollution has sullied (or destroyed) plankton, the traditional food of many shellfish. If you are what you eat, then these shellfish have been raised on a starvation diet, and their flavor has suffered as a result.

Shellfish are excellent choices for the busy cook because all types cook in a matter of minutes. Like fish, their flesh is naturally tender. And like fish, shellfish can be ruined by careless treatment. Cook shrimps or scallops too long and they become rubbery. Crabmeat and mussels lose flavor, and lobster becomes tough. But cook shellfish carefully and you will enjoy flavors that evoke the essence of the sea.

Most types of shellfish are available the year round, although oysters are traditionally eaten during the winter because they spawn during the warmer months. (At that time some people consider their flavor and texture to be less satisfactory.) The tiny Maine shrimps, which have a sweet flavor matched only by their counterparts in Scandinavia, are also seasonal (winter). It's a rare fish market, however, that doesn't stock at least some kind of shellfish at all times.

When you're selecting shellfish, the most important factor is to find out where they originated. Everyone has heard a horror story about someone who ate raw clams and came down with hepatitis. It's foolish to take a chance on eating shellfish that might have come from contaminated waters. Bivalve mollusks, such as mussels, clams, and oysters, retain the toxins found in their environments, so it's particularly important to determine where these shellfish originate.

Only buy from a fishmonger who stocks shellfish from clean waters. If you are suspicious about where the shellfish originated, ask to see the health tags attached to the packing crates, because shellfish gathered in certified clean areas are tagged by the appropriate state inspection agency. Smell the shellfish before you take them home, and if they have any off odor whatsoever, march right back to the fishmonger and demand a refund.

Many people limit their consumption of shellfish because they have heard that all shellfish contain high amounts of cholesterol. That's not so. In the past, testing methods were used that inaccurately measured the amount of cholesterol in shellfish. The new testing uses gas chromatography which has shown that about 40 percent of the sterols in filter-feeding shellfish is cholesterol and the other 60 percent is plant sterols, which are not harmful to our health. What this means is that any shellfish that eat algae, such as oysters, clams, mussels, and scallops, are low in cholesterol. Lobsters, shrimp, crabs, and squid, on the other hand, feed on other forms of animal life and have higher cholesterol levels.

Try to use shellfish the day you purchase them. As with fish, if shellfish are kept too long before cooking, they lose moisture. A really fresh oyster, for example, is chock-full of liquid. When you open one that is dried out, you know that it is either old or has been stored on its side so that the liquid has drained out. Either way, it's an inferior oyster and should be discarded.

Clams

A seaside clambake is a traditional New England ritual, where prodigious numbers of clams and lobsters are cooked in a pit dug in the sand. Preparation for a clambake starts hours before the actual cooking when the pit is lined with large stones, then filled with firewood that burns down to coals and heats the stones. Once the stones are hot enough, the pit is layered with wet seaweed, clams, lobsters, corn—and even chicken—that steam in the heat retained by the stones. Steamed clams, lobsters, and all the trimmings make the meal that generations of New Englanders have proclaimed the ideal choice for a summer day on the beach.

Clambakes have been part of the American culinary experience ever since the Indians taught the Pilgrims how to steam shellfish in seaweed. The Pilgrims were using what was once one of the most abundant foods in the New World. Several kinds of clams are indigenous to America, the most common of which are the hard- and soft-shell types. Around here, hard-shell clams, gathered by raking or dredging below the low tide level, are often called by their Indian name of *quahog* (pronounced co-hog). As large quahogs have a tough texture, they're best chopped up for chowder or stuffing, while the smaller clams, known as littlenecks and cherrystones, are tender enough to eat raw. Littleneck clams run about 2 to 2½ inches long, while cherrystones are a little larger, about 2½ to 3 inches long. Quahogs generally range from 3 to 6 inches.

Soft-shell clams, more commonly known as steamers, burrow into mud or sand near to shore and are gathered at low tide when their airholes are visible. If you've ever gone clamming, it's probably soft-shell clams that you've gathered by the bucket. The texture of soft-shell clams is softer than that of the hard-shells, but they tend to be sandy.

When we started Legal Sea Foods, clams were a common, inexpensive commodity. But pollution and overharvesting have taken their toll. The growing scarcity of clams has prompted some companies to start cultivating hard-shell clams as a commercial crop. Under ideal conditions, a hard-shell clam will mature in three years, rather than the five to eight years it would take in the wild. These businesses raise the clams in a hatchery for four to six months, and then transfer them to a protected area where the clams complete their growing cycles.

At the restaurants, we keep our clam offerings simple. Perhaps our best-known clam dish is our chowder—which owes its hearty flavor to generous amounts of hard-shell clams and cream, but many customers opt for our fried or steamed soft-shell clams. If you're uncertain about which type of clam to buy, remember that for frying and steaming, steamer or soft-shell clams would be your choice, while for stuffings, chowders, or raw clams, select hard-shell clams.

Clams will live for days after they are dug, but they must be stored properly under cool conditions. If clams have been shipped, they should have been layered flat to keep their juices from escaping. If you find a soft-shell clam with its neck hanging limply out of its shell, discard it. It is dead. Really fresh clams have tightly closed shells. When in doubt, poke the end of the clam's neck. A clam that is alive will move its neck slightly.

Hard-shell clams are rarely gritty, but if you are preparing steamers you will want to clean them as thoroughly as possible before cooking. You have probably heard that clams will disgorge their grit when soaked in water with a sprinkling of cornmeal on top. I don't know where this old wives' tale originated; not only will the clams fail to purify themselves, but also if they stay long enough in the fresh water, they will die.

The only way to deal with sandy steamers is to clean their shells with a stiff kitchen brush, rinsing each one off before placing it in the steaming pot, and then, once they are steamed, to take some of the clam broth and serve it along with the clams. You dip the steamed clam first into the broth to clean it, and then into melted butter. If you are frying clams, remember that the grit is found in the clams' bellies. Some fishmongers sell clam strips—which are the grit-free necks. A little sand doesn't bother me. I eat clams whole—whatever sand they contain is minimum —and easily compensated for by their delicious flavor.

Crabs

Many people prefer the delicate, sweet taste of crabmeat to that of lobster. Crabs come in all sizes, but you have to work for your crabmeat pleasures if you live in New England, where the crabs are small and the pickings are slim.

The blue crab, the most common variety found in New England, is available fresh during the summer months. Extracting the meat is such a tedious process (and so few shops stock fresh crabs) that you're better off buying the picked fresh crabmeat sold in refrigerated containers. One caution—this crabmeat is exceptionally perishable and should be used immediately.

Blue crabs are not unique to New England. In fact, the soft-shell crabs of Maryland and Virginia are blue crabs in transition. During molting season (the time when the crabs shed their hard shells) their new shells are paper thin. At this point almost the entire crab is edible. I consider soft-shell crabs to be a unique American delicacy—almost like Dublin Bay prawns in Ireland. They're delicious either deep-fried or sautéed in butter. All you need to do is to clean them, and cook them carefully. The live crabs are air shipped to many parts of the country in season, or you can buy them frozen.

Cleaning Soft-Shell Crabs

You can't be squeamish about cleaning soft-shell crabs, because you cut them up while they're alive. Be assured, however, that they have an elementary nervous system, and after the first cut, they are dead. (If you are tempted to stop reading here, ask your fishmonger to dress the crabs for you.)

A pair of kitchen shears is essential for removing the eyes, mouth, and gills. Numb the crabs by placing them in the freezer spread out on a jelly-roll pan for about five minutes. If you wait any longer, they will freeze to death. Take the crabs, place them on the counter, and cut them across the face at an upward angle to remove the eye sockets and the lower mouth. Then, lift up the apron and trim off the gills. Cut off the tail-like apron. Everything remaining is edible.

Stone crabs from Florida are another seasonal delicacy. They're unique because you eat only one leg rather than the entire crab. When the crab is caught, one leg is removed, and the crab is tossed back in the water where it will regenerate another leg. The name comes from the shell, which is so hard that you'll need a hammer or mallet to crack it. Stone crabs may be served hot or cold. I think they're best with a mustard sauce.

Until recently, we served about one hundred thousand pounds of Alaskan king crab at the restaurants yearly. Now, we use about 10 percent of the amount we bought five years ago because this crab has become very scarce. It's a pity, because Alaskan king crab is meaty and good-tasting. Don't confuse Alaskan crab with the delicious Dungeness crab, also found on the Pacific Coast. The Dungeness crab has a finer texture and flavor than the Alaskan crab, but it is rarely shipped outside of its boundaries.

The scarcity of Alaskan king crab has inspired the Japanese to come up with an imitation version. They process pollock, press it into crab-leg shapes, and sell it as imitation crabmeat. Don't expect any real flavor or nutrition from this high-class junk food, because many of the nutrients have been leached out in the processing. At first glance this product may appear to be less expensive than the real thing—but when you realize that it is nothing more than fiber with chemical additives, you'll opt for something else. I have never sold imitation crabmeat and never intend to.

Lobsters

Practically every tourist who visits Boston wants to sample a Maine lobster. These blue-black crustaceans, considered the prime delicacy of the shellfish family, were once so plentiful that New England fishermen used them as bait. Now, connoisseurs around the world have discovered the sweet taste of *Homarus americanus,* the native North American lobster—and the supply barely keeps up with the demand.

We sell so many lobsters that I finally built special lobster storage tanks at our commissary. (At any time, we have any-where from 20,000 to 40,000 pounds of lobster on hand.) This way I'm able to count on a continuous supply of lobsters and to guarantee that the lobsters we sell are held under optimum conditions. Some local dealers store lobsters in harbor water. About the only good thing you can say about this water is that it contains salt—I don't like to think about the other elements it contains.

At Legal, we make special storage water out of drinking water, salt, and minerals carefully formulated to match the composition of ocean water. The lobsters held in this water retain a higher quality than those kept under more haphazard conditions.

Next time you eat a lobster, consider the number of years it spent growing large enough for you to enjoy. It takes five to eight years, for example, for a lobster to reach one pound in weight. Most people believe that it's illegal to catch a lobster that weighs less than one pound, but size rather than weight is actually the determining factor. A lobster weighs about one pound when it measures 3 3/16 inches from its eye sockets to the end of its main body segment (known as the carapace), and so this measurement has been adopted by most coastal states from Maine to Florida as the minimum legal size for a lobster. There are, however, no restrictions affecting the sale of large lobsters. I always keep a few large lobsters on hand for customers with king-sized appetites. It's not unusual for members of the New England Patriots football team to come into our Park Plaza restaurant in Boston and polish off thirteen-pound lobsters at one sitting.

Most people, however, prefer lobsters that weigh between 1 1/2 and 2 pounds. Lobsters are graded by weight. Massachusetts grades its lobsters down to 1/8-pound differences, but most merchants don't bother with those fractions. The grades you're most likely to see are a "chicken" or "chix" lobster weighing in at 1 pound; a "quarter," 1 1/8 to 1 1/4 pounds; "select," 1 1/4 to 1 3/4; "deuces or 2 pounds," 1 3/4 to 2 pounds; "small jumbo," 2 1/4 to 2 1/2; and "jumbo," more than 2 1/2 pounds.

You might expect that the smaller the lobster, the more tender the meat, but that's not necessarily so. A lobster moves by pushing its tail backward through the water. If it flips its tail often enough, its meat can become tough. A baby chicken lobster moves around constantly, while an older (and larger) lobster is more likely to spend time sitting around and eating. When you eat a ten-pound lobster you benefit from its indolence—big chunks of meat. However, at a certain point lobsters age and their flesh loses consistency and becomes almost stringy in texture. That's why I don't recommend buying a lobster larger than fifteen pounds. My ideal lobster would weigh between three and four pounds. At that weight there's plenty of meat, and the lobster is still tender. (Regardless of the size, don't expect lobster to taste as tender as fish, because lobster flesh is chewier and tougher than almost any fish you can buy.)

Buy live lobsters only. An ideal lobster should be blue-black in color and active; its tail should curve under its body when you pick it up, not hang flaccidly. If the lobster seems sluggish, watch out—it is probably near death, which is a problem, because a dead lobster spoils quickly, and its meat disintegrates in texture and becomes almost like sawdust. During molting season in summer the lobster contains far less meat than at other times of the year. A lobster grows by shedding its shell, and at that time its shell is soft and its meat is less palatable. After a couple of weeks the shell firms up, but it takes a month or two for the meat to regain consistency. That's why if you're given a choice between buying hard- or soft-shell lobsters, select hard-shell because they contain far more meat with a better consistency.

The easiest way to distinguish between a hard- and a soft-shell lobster is to grab it by the back of the shell. Then squeeze the shell with your thumb and forefinger; a hard shell will stay rigid, while a soft shell will give a little.

If you don't want to serve the lobster immediately, it's possible to keep it in the refrigerator overnight. The lobster will stay in good condition for twelve to eighteen hours if placed in a paper bag with holes punched in it. Adding seaweed also helps preserve the lobster. Under no circumstances store a lobster in fresh water, such as in the bathtub, because it will drown in fresh water.

Eating a Lobster

Those of us in New England take it for granted that everyone knows how to eat a lobster, but of course that's not so. The ritual of eating a lobster starts by covering yourself with an apron, or having plenty of towels on hand, because it is a messy process.

Nutcrackers work well for cracking the lobster's shell, which varies in density. The shell of a lobster before molting may be so hard that you'll need a hammer to crack it, while after molting, the lobster's soft shell is pliable and can be easily torn apart with your fingers or cracked with a nutcracker, or pliers.

Remove the large claws and crack the shells. Holding the lobster in one hand, grab the tail with your other hand and bend the tail until it breaks free.

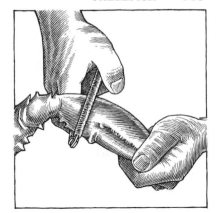

Then, using kitchen shears or a knife, slice through the soft shell on the underside of the lobster so the meat is easily removed.

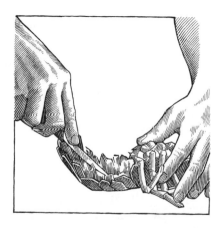

People often stop eating a lobster after they have savored the tail and claw meat, but I think some of the most tender meat is contained in the lobster's body. Hold the body with the eyes facing down and pull on both sides of the shell where the body cavity opens. The upper part of the shell will break off, leaving you with the meat contained between the cartilages.

A boiled lobster contains quite a bit of water in the chest cavity. If you want to keep the lobster whole for appearance's sake, pierce the underside of the lobster at the point where the chest cavity meets the body and let it drain. Otherwise, twist the tail from the chest so that the water can drain out of the chest cavity.

Save the soft green substance contained within the cavity. That's the lobster's liver (known as tomalley) and it is delicious dipped into butter or spread on a cracker. You may also find some red roe (female lobster's eggs), which are also edible.

Discard the stomach sac in the head found right behind the eyes, and the feathery gills above the cartilage. A nutpick is useful to extract the tender meat found between the cartilages. The easiest way to enjoy the meat in the little legs is to pull the pieces through your teeth to squeeze it out.

Dip the lobster meat into drawn butter—or eat it plain with a squeeze of lemon or lime juice. Once you've done this, you'll understand why people from all over the world savor New England lobster.

You won't find many lobster recipes in this book. Like other New Englanders, I prefer my lobster cooked simply. I think a fresh boiled lobster is the ultimate lobster preparation, but you may wish to experiment. Cook lobster any way you wish, but leave it in the spotlight. Lobster tastes best when its sweet flavor is not overshadowed by other ingredients.

Mussels

A few years ago, you couldn't give mussels away. These shiny blue-black mollusks, beloved by generations of French cooks, had few advocates in America. Most cooks wouldn't eat mussels, and when they did get adventurous and tried them, too often the mussels were puny and filled with grit.

Fortunately, Americans are beginning to realize that mussels are one of the great shellfish choices. They're flavorful, tender, and—like other shellfish—low in calories. I like to think that restaurants like ours, where mussels are prominently featured on the menu, have converted skeptics into believers. Of equal import, however, is the improvement in the quality of mussels we are able to buy.

Entrepreneurs in Maine and other parts of New England are cultivating mussels commercially. These farmed, or cultured, mussels are superior in quality to those harvested in the wild.

Wild mussels are intertidal mollusks that spend half of their lives out of the water exposed to the elements. Under these conditions, mussels may take eight or nine years to become large enough to eat. During the winter months, when the weather is harsh, the mussels develop thick shells rather than plump bodies.

Cultivated mussels are either grown on lines or webbing suspended in clean, sheltered waters, or they are seeded on the bottom of the ocean floor in sheltered spots. Either procedure provides more favorable conditions for mussel development than the vagaries of the wild. When mussels are grown under cultivated conditions they will reach full size in three years. One bonus of rapid cultivation is that these mussels are free from the pearls (calcified deposits) that build up in wild mussels when so many years pass before they are gathered.

Once the mussels are harvested, they are put through a cleaning process. The mussels are plunged into tanks where they siphon purified water, thereby eliminating much of the grit in their systems. (An average-sized mussel siphons about eighteen gallons of water a day in its search for food.) Then they are separated by size and are ready for the market.

At Legal Sea Foods we buy only these cultured mussels. I think they're worth the extra cost we pay, and suggest that you also seek out a fishmonger who stocks them. Be sure to check with your fishmonger about the season when the mussels spawn, because during those months their flesh is leaner. (In the summer, we shift from Maine mussels to Cape Cod mussels, which have a different spawning cycle.)

Sometimes the mussel shells are gaping open when you buy them. This is not a sure sign that the mussels are dead, but smell them and discard any with an off odor. Unfortunately, even one spoiled mussel can contaminate mussels stored nearby, so you may have to throw out a whole batch if you detect spoilage. Try storing mussels in a colander, so that if one mussel is bad, its juice will drain out rather than contaminating all the mussels around it.

I think mussels' delicate flavor is best appreciated when they are prepared simply. Steamed mussels are perennial favorites at our restaurants, as is our Mussels au Gratin appetizer. Mussels are also an excellent ingredient in seafood pastas—or cold shellfish salads. It is important, however, that they be cooked just to the point when they open. If any mussels remain closed after cooking, discard them. When they are overcooked, mussels drastically lose flavor and shrivel up. Treat mussels gently, and you will retain the qualities that have made them a favorite of European cooks for aeons.

We use mussels about 2 inches long in our restaurants. Smaller than that, it requires too much manpower to extract a small amount of meat. To clean mussels, scrub their shells with a stiff brush to dislodge any mud or barnacles. (Cultivated mussels will need less effort.)

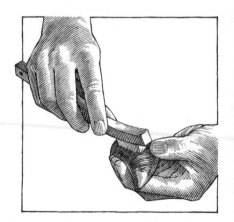

Mussels attach themselves to rocks with a beardlike substance called a byssus. It's easily removed by holding the mussel in one hand and the byssus in the other and yanking up with a swift motion—or you can remove it with a knife.

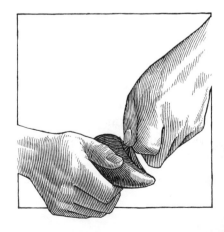

Oysters

A good oyster has a fresh, briny taste that is the essence of the sea. Many people prefer to savor oysters raw on the half shell, but they're also delicious dipped in a batter and fried, cooked up in a simple stew, baked in a sauce, or used as a stuffing ingredient for fish or poultry.

Oysters are found in the shallow waters along the coast of the North American continent. The oysters we harvest in this region range from two to four inches long, while those from the West Coast tend to be larger, except for the tiny Olympia oysters from Puget Sound in Washington State.

The size and taste of oysters varies depending upon the location in which they grow. Some local connoisseurs claim they can taste the difference between oysters harvested in Cotuit, and those from Wellfleet—a few miles away. We serve both kinds in our restaurants, where our customers enjoy them equally.

For centuries, people have eaten oysters as an aphrodisiac. Like many a piece of folklore, this has a basis in fact. New England oysters have an unusually high zinc content, an element that affects sexual potency, among other things. West Coast oysters, on the other hand, contain less zinc, and, I think, are less flavorful.

When you're selecting oysters, pick those that are tightly closed and smell fresh. If they have an off odor—either closed or open—the oysters are spoiled and should be discarded. Properly packed oysters will last in storage about a month, but they should be packed top side up and stored flat. If they are packed sideways they lose their liquid and spoil faster.

Shucking Oysters

Shucking oysters (removing their shells) is not difficult to do, but takes a certain amount of practice. The thickness of the shells depends on the variety. For example, the Belon oysters that are native to France are now being harvested in Maine. These oysters are difficult to shuck because they have a thin, delicate shell that breaks easily when you try to open it.

You should always protect your hands with cloth or rubber kitchen gloves. I once cut a tendon in my right hand shucking oysters. (I was in a hurry, and the knife slipped off the oyster and into my hand.) You should also use an oyster knife, a tool that can be found in many fish markets or kitchen-supply stores.

The fresher the oyster, the more difficult it is to open. One trick I've found useful is to heat the oysters in a hot oven for a few seconds. You don't want to cook them—just heat their shells. Or, you could place the oysters in the freezer for about five minutes, which also lulls them into relaxing their muscles.

I'm going to give you two ways to shuck oysters. Holding the oyster in one hand and opening it with the other is the faster way to open an oyster, but beginners may prefer to use the towel technique while they are learning. The way you open an oyster doesn't matter—just try not to mutilate its flesh in the process.

Take an oyster and place the curved part of its shell in the palm of your hand. The halves of the oyster shell are tightly closed, and it can be difficult to pry them apart with a knife. Decide where the seam is, insert the point of the knife into it, and wriggle the knife. If you are successful, the oyster shell will open a crack, and you will be able to finish the process using your hand.

While you are maneuvering the oyster, be sure to hold it level so that you don't lose the liquid.

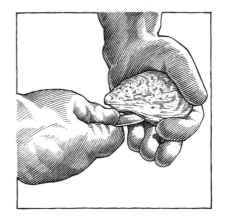

Next, run the knife along the top shell to release the oyster into the bottom half of the shell. Pull off the top shell and discard it. Scoop out the oyster flesh with the knife.

If this process makes you a little nervous, try what I call the towel technique. All this means is that you use a kitchen towel to hold the oyster. Shield your hand with a kitchen towel, grasp the oyster, and hold it down on the kitchen counter—the towel will keep it from slipping. If you have a hard time finding the seam, look for the back of the oyster where the hinge is. Insert the knife in the hinge and pry up the shell to separate the top from the bottom shell. Then, follow the instructions above.

Raw oysters, served on the half shell with cocktail sauce and a lemon wedge for squeezing, is the number one oyster preparation at our restaurants. I think that's the best way to savor oysters' fresh, briny flavor. Oyster stew, however, is a knockout; so are stuffed oysters.

Scallops

I think scallops are one of the most versatile kinds of shellfish. Regardless of how you cook them—baked, broiled, deep-fried, or sautéed—scallops stay tender in every way. Their tenderness is surprising because what we think of as the whole scallop is just the scallop's muscle. This muscle develops to a disproportionate size because a scallop goes through the water by moving its shells together, expelling a jet of water. (The shells often contain roe, which is quite a delicacy—a fact the French know well.

Unfortunately, in America the fishermen throw the roe away with the shells when they shuck the scallops.)

There are basically two kinds of scallops: large sea scallops caught 150 miles out at sea, that are available the year round, and tiny bay—or Cape—scallops, that live in the shallow coastal waters and are usually available during the winter months.

Bay scallops never grow into sea scallops, they're a completely different type of scallop. The bay scallops we harvest off Cape Cod live in waters that are continually flushed with high tides, which helps keep the water unpolluted. For some reason the sugar content seems to be higher in scallops that have the good feed resulting from unpolluted waters. When you cook Cape scallops they brown quickly and taste almost sugary. As they get older, they lose that sweet flavor, and take longer to brown. That's one way to tell whether or not they are fresh. Scallops from other parts of the country never brown as fast, and never seem to have as much flavor.

Like other shellfish, bay scallops are now being harvested commercially. The growers close down the beds when it gets too cold and remove the scallops from the water for the season. It makes sense to grow scallops commercially because if they are not harvested after a couple of years, they die.

Some markets sell Calico Bay scallops, found in the Florida area and shipped up here. I don't stock Calico scallops because they are already slightly cooked by the time they reach the consumer. These scallops are so tiny that in order to open them easily, the processors steam them for a few moments. In the process, the scallops lose a lot of their juices, and end up lacking the flavor they once had.

Most markets sell fresh scallops, which are far preferable to the frozen kind. If you live in an area where markets stock only frozen scallops, cook them while they are still partially frozen. Once they thaw out completely, the scallops have lost too much of their juices. One caution. Some purveyors soak shucked scallops in water or a phosphate solution. This increases the volume by almost a third and whitens the flesh, but depletes the flavor.

Scallops cook almost immediately—a fact most people ignore. When scallops are overcooked, they develop a rubbery texture. Bay scallops particularly suffer from poor cooking procedures because of their tiny size.

Shrimp

Shrimp are the most popular shellfish we serve at Legal Sea Foods—and probably the most popular shellfish in America. Shrimp taste good, it's true, but part of the reason they're so popular is that they're a known quantity. No matter where you travel, you're likely to find some form of shrimp, because they're caught in every ocean around the world. Shrimp have the added advantage of freezing well. Unlike most other shellfish, shrimp have enough body texture so that they don't deteriorate when frozen.

Buying shrimp can be confusing. As a rule of thumb, remember that the larger the size, the higher the price. The most expensive shrimp are jumbo-sized, no more than ten per pound. Average-sized shrimp are about fifteen to twenty per pound, and smaller shrimp twenty-one to twenty-five per pound. Of course, shrimp continue to be graded in size as they get smaller, but most retail shops don't stock the smallest-sized shrimp. (There is a big price break for shrimp that fall in the thirty-one to thirty-five per pound category.)

Most of the shrimp consumed in New England—and the rest of the country—are frozen shrimp shipped up from Louisiana, Florida, and other southern states. However, many of the largest-sized shrimp you find at supermarkets and fishmongers come from the west coast of Mexico. These shrimp seem to have a longer shelf life, but are not as tender as the American Gulf shrimp. Chinese restaurants, for example, tend to use them because of their long shelf life.

New Englanders do have their own native shrimp—the succulent, tiny Maine shrimp available during the winter months. These shrimp are a great delicacy, but they're highly perishable, and their texture is softer than that of most shrimp, so they freeze poorly. If you're able to locate a source for fresh Maine shrimp, keep in mind that they cook literally in seconds. I think they're best boiled for about twenty seconds, and then plunged into cold water to stop the cooking process. When you overcook these shrimp they become mushy and tasteless, but cooked right they are an excellent addition to seafood salads or Scandinavian-style open-faced sandwiches.

The caveat not to overcook shrimp is not limited to Maine shrimp. Most people overcook shrimp—they figure that if a recipe calls for two minutes, three or four minutes is even better. When you overcook the Gulf varieties of shrimp, their texture toughens and they lose flavor. Shrimp are cooked when they turn pink, and their texture becomes firm. Two minutes is long enough to boil medium-sized shrimp—longer than that and you'll destroy their texture and leach out their flavor. It's also unnecessary to remove the black veins that run down the back of shrimp. Removing the veins is purely an aesthetic judgment. You have to decide whether removing them improves their appearance sufficiently to counter the fact that you've probably massacred the shape of the shrimp in the process. The veins have no taste, and I see no reason to remove them.

Unless you're lucky enough to live near one of the shrimping areas, the shrimp you buy will have been previously frozen. Regardless of whether they are fresh or frozen, shrimp should have a nice, shiny sheen. When shrimp have been standing in the store case too long they appear dull. Good-quality shrimp also should look clean, with no dark marks on their shells.

The shrimp should smell fresh. If there is any off odor, the shrimp are old and you shouldn't buy them. There are three kinds of shrimp: white, pink, and brown. You don't have to know more than the fact that white shrimp have the most delicate flavor, and brown shrimp often possess an iodine aftertaste. Chain stores often carry brown shrimp because they cost less than white shrimp.

An iodine aftertaste may be unpleasant, but it doesn't mean that the shrimp have spoiled, but rather that their food has a high iodine content. (This is the same taste you also can get with sole and flounder, which are bottom-feeding fish.) There is a difference between iodine and ammonia odors, however, and you should learn to tell them apart. Iodine has a medicinal odor, while ammonia smells bad—almost like chemicals. If shrimp smell—or taste—like ammonia, toss them out. They are old and on the verge of spoiling.

Shrimp lend themselves to all kinds of cooking. A steamed shrimp cocktail is a perennial favorite, but we also serve shrimp broiled with garlic, fried, or even layered in a casserole with mushrooms. In a few more pages I'll describe our favorite recipes from the restaurants, as well as a few extra recipes for this, the most popular of shellfish.

Squid

Believe it or not, squid are shellfish, although they resemble throwbacks to science fiction monsters with the way they look and move. Squid have plasticlike internal shells known as quills (or pens) rather than external shells. Squid also contain ink sacs filled with a black fluid that is ejected through a siphon that clouds the water, allowing them to escape from enemies. Although squid move through the water using their fins, they also use their siphons to eject water and travel in the opposite direction. Their eyes dart in all directions, so they can see their enemies easily.

People in the Mediterranean countries, such as Italy, Spain, and Greece, utilize squid to the fullest, but Americans have been slow to appreciate what good-tasting and versatile shellfish they are.

The problem lies as much in the way people cook squid as in its appearance. Most people overcook squid by a factor of ten. Squid has a firm texture to begin with, and when it is overcooked, the texture becomes like rubber bands. Squid should be cooked for a few minutes; in fact, fried squid should cook less than one minute.

You can pick out fresh squid by its color, which is creamy. Don't buy pinkish-colored squid—it is old. Fresh squid tastes bland, so I think frying it is the best cooking choice. It is also delicious as part of a marinated salad—or stuffed and braised in a liquid.

Cleaning Squid

Many fishmongers will clean whole squid for you, but it's easy to do at home. All you need is a knife and a spot near a sink so you can rinse the squid and the countertop as you're working.

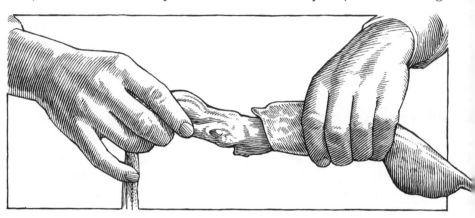

Lay a squid down on a counter. Holding the body with one hand, grasp the head and the tentacles firmly with the other hand and pull outward. The head, tentacles, and pulpy intestines will detach from the body (sometimes called the hood).

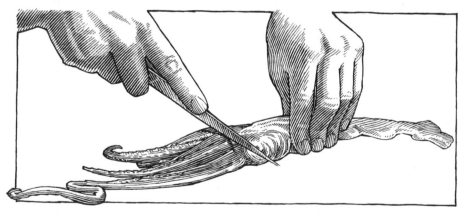

Cut off the eyes and intestines from the tentacles and toss them out. Unless you want to save the ink sac for a sauce, discard it as well.

Examine the tentacles. At the point where they are attached to the head you will notice a brown hard mass smaller than a fingernail. This is the mouth. Squeeze this part of the tentacles and the mouth will pop out. Discard it. You will be left with a tubelike body cavity and the tentacles, both of which are edible.

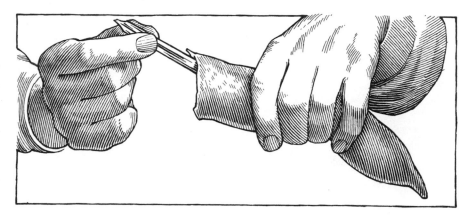

Insert your hand into the body cavity and pull out any remaining intestines as well as the transparent bone. Rinse out the body cavity. Place the body on the countertop and scrape off the grayish skin with a knife blade. This is easy to do; after the initial scrape, usually the rest of the skin peels right off.

If you wish a tubular presentation, detach the fins attached along the bottom half of the squid, making sure you do not puncture the body cavity. Otherwise, leave them on. Once you have rinsed and dried the squid, it is ready to cook.

Shellfish Recipes

Clams

Clam Chowder

I think our clam chowder is the best in the business—and the public certainly agrees. We sell about seven hundred gallons of clam chowder each week at our restaurants and take-out counters. The reason for its popularity is simple. We use only the best ingredients and plenty of them. Don't try and economize by cutting back on the amount of clams or cream because the chowder will never taste as flavorful as ours.

4 quarts littleneck clams (about 1²/₃ cups cooked and
   chopped)
1 clove garlic, chopped
1 cup water
2 ounces salt pork, finely chopped
2 cups chopped onions
3 tablespoons flour
1 1/2 pounds potatoes, peeled, and diced into 1/2-inch cubes
4 1/2 cups clam broth
3 cups Fish Stock
2 cups light cream
Oyster crackers (optional)

Clean the clams and place them in a large pot along with the garlic and water. Steam the clams just until opened, about 6 to 10 minutes, depending upon their size. Drain and shell the clams, reserving the broth. Mince the clam flesh, and set aside. Filter the clam broth either through coffee filters or cheesecloth and set aside.

In a large, heavy pot slowly render the salt pork. Remove the cracklings and set them aside. Slowly cook the onions in the fat for about 6 minutes, stirring frequently, or until cooked through but not browned. Stir in the flour and cook, stirring, for 3 minutes. Add the reserved clam broth and Fish Stock, and whisk to remove any flour lumps. Bring the liquid to a boil, add the potatoes, lower the heat, and simmer until the potatoes are cooked through, about 15 minutes.

Stir in the reserved clams, salt-pork cracklings, and light cream. Heat the chowder until it is the temperature you prefer. Serve in large soup bowls with oyster crackers on the side. (Serves 8)

Steamed Clams with Garlic-Parsley Butter

Steamed clams are delicious served as simply as possible—with melted butter and lots of French bread to mop up the broth. This garlic-parsley butter, however, is a flavorful alternative to plain melted butter. Be sure to melt the butter slowly so that it absorbs the taste of the garlic. If you have any leftover clam juice, strain it through coffee filters and store in the freezer to substitute for fish stock in recipes.

    5 pounds steamer clams
    1/2 pound butter
    1 tablespoon minced garlic
    1/4 cup minced parsley

Wash the clams thoroughly to remove any grit or mud. Place them in a deep pot and add water about 3/4 to 1 inch deep up the sides of the pot. Cover the pot, bring the water to a boil, lower the heat slightly, and cook rapidly for about 5 to 8 minutes, or until the shells open indicating that the clams are cooked. Discard any clams with closed shells. Check after 5 minutes, because you don't want the clams to overcook.

Meanwhile, place the butter and garlic in a small saucepan and slowly melt the butter. Let the garlic stew in the melted butter while the clams continue to cook. Just before serving, add the minced parsley.

To serve, place the clams on a large platter, and place the garlic-parsley dip in small bowls. Strain some of the clam juice into bowls.

As you eat each clam, remove the dark membrane around its neck and toss it out. Dip the clam first into the clam broth and then into the garlic-parsley butter. (Serves 4)

Crabs

Sautéed Soft-Shell Crabs

Cooked this way, the crabs retain their delicate flavor. Count on two to three crabs per serving, depending upon their size.

    8–12 soft-shell crabs (about 2 pounds), cleaned (see page
      109)
    1/2 cup buttermilk
    1 cup flour
    1/2 teaspoon salt
    6 tablespoons butter
    2 tablespoons vegetable oil
    Lemon wedges

Soak the crabs in the buttermilk for at least 30 minutes. Mix the flour and salt together in a large bowl.

Remove the crabs from the buttermilk, coat them with flour, and shake to remove any excess.

Heat the butter and oil together in a large frying pan. If you have a 12- to 15-inch pan you should be able to sauté the crabs all at once. Otherwise preheat the oven to 250 degrees and as the crabs are cooked place them on a cookie sheet lined with a paper bag and keep them warm in the oven. (If you overcrowd the pan the crabs will not brown evenly.)

Sauté the crabs in the butter mixture, turning once. They should be lightly browned and cooked through in 4 to 5 minutes.

Serve immediately accompanied by lemon wedges to squeeze over the crabs as you eat them. (Serves 4)

VARIATION: Brown slivered blanched almonds in butter and pour over the crabs before serving.

Crabmeat Roll

Fresh New England crabmeat has a sweet, delicate flavor best accentuated with homemade mayonnaise and nothing else. Never sprinkle with paprika, which masks the taste.

    1 pound fresh crabmeat
    1/3 cup Easy Blender Mayonnaise
    4–6 hotdog buns
    Butter

Pick over the crabmeat to remove any pieces of cartilage. Press down on the crabmeat slightly to remove excess liquid, and mix with the mayonnaise.

Butter the outside of the hotdog buns and sauté over medium heat until they are toasted. Stuff the buns with the crabmeat, and serve immediately (Serves 4 to 6)

Deviled Crab

This is a good way to use frozen Alaskan king crabs. Soak them in water for about thirty minutes before using, because these crabs are packed in a salt brine and will be unbearably salty unless you leach out some of the salt before cooking them.

    4 tablespoons butter
    1 medium onion, chopped
    2/3 cup chopped celery
    2/3 cup chopped green pepper
    1/3 cup chopped parsley
    3/4 pound lump crabmeat (or 2 pounds of king crab in the
       shell)
    1/3 cup mayonnaise
    Dash of Worcestershire sauce
    Dash of cayenne pepper
    Cracker Crumb Mixture or bread crumbs

Preheat the oven to 400 degrees. Heat 3 tablespoons of the butter in a large frying pan and sauté the onions, celery, and green pepper for about 5 minutes, stirring frequently. Remove from the heat and cool slightly. Stir in the parsley, crabmeat, and mayonnaise. Taste and season with Worcestershire sauce and cayenne pepper.

Spread in a buttered baking dish and sprinkle with the Cracker Crumb Mixture. Dot with the remaining 1 tablespoon butter. Bake for about 15 minutes, or until the crabmeat is heated through. Serve immediately. (Serves 4)

Crabmeat with Tomatoes

This easy brunch recipe, made with fresh crabmeat, takes about five minutes to prepare.

    4 English muffins
    1/3–1/2 cup Easy Blender Mayonnaise
    1 pound fresh crabmeat
    2 large, meaty tomatoes, such as beefsteak, thickly sliced
    1/2 cup grated Monterey Jack cheese

Preheat the broiler. Split the muffins. Toast them and let them cool.

Lightly spread each muffin half with mayonnaise. Combine the remaining mayonnaise with the crabmeat. Place a tomato slice on each muffin half and top with the crabmeat. Sprinkle with the cheese.

Put the muffins on a broiling pan and broil for about 5 minutes, or until the cheese melts. Serve immediately. (Serves 4)

Pasta with Crabmeat Sauce

This preparation accentuates the delicate flavor of East Coast crabmeat.

    2 cups heavy cream
    2 tablespoons butter
    2 tablespoons chopped ripe tomato, peeled and seeded
    1/2 teaspoon Dijon mustard
    1/3 cup freshly grated Parmesan cheese
    1 pound fresh crabmeat
    1 pound fettuccine or linguine noodles

Before boiling the pasta, start the sauce. Combine the cream and butter in a saucepan, and gently boil for 8 minutes. Add the tomato and cook for 2 minutes longer, or until the mixture has reduced and thickened slightly. Add the mustard, cheese, and crabmeat, and cook 1 minute longer.

Meanwhile, cook the pasta al dente.

Drain the pasta, and toss with the crabmeat sauce. Serve immediately. (Serves 4)

VARIATION: *Scallops with Pasta.* Substitute 3/4 pound thinly sliced steamed scallops for the crabmeat, and add 1/2 cup of the scallop-steaming juices to the cream before reducing it.

Lobster

Boiled Lobster

Boiling lobster is one of those cooking skills that sounds elementary, but there are a few tips you should know before dumping the lobsters in a pot and calling it quits.

Most lobsters cook much faster than you might expect. We've worked out a timetable for the restaurants that works well as a general rule. Keep in mind that all timing should be done from the moment the water comes to a *second boil.* Here's the timing we use:

1 to 1½ pounds	10 to 12 minutes
1½ to 2 pounds	15 to 18 minutes
2½ to 5 pounds	20 to 25 minutes
6 to 10 pounds	25 to 35 minutes
10 to 15 pounds	35 to 40 minutes
15 to 20 pounds	60 minutes

An exception to this timing is hard-shell lobsters, which take about 5 minutes a pound longer to cook. Also, the claws on a large lobster will need more time to cook than the body, so you might wish to start them about 5 minutes sooner.

We serve our lobsters with drawn butter, which is butter melted just to the point where it begins to boil then removed from the heat and served warm.

Water
4 1¼ pound lobsters
10 tablespoons drawn butter

Fill a large pot with cold water, bring it to a boil, and immediately add the lobsters. When the water comes to a second boil, lower the heat to a gentle boil and start timing.

Remove the lobsters from the water, let them drain for a minute or two, and serve along with drawn butter and lots of towels. If you've never eaten lobster, the illustrations on page 113 should make it an easy procedure. Eating lobster is messy, so provide plenty of napkins. (Serves 4)

Lobster Salad

Here in New England we think that the best way to serve lobster is the simplest way. The delicate flavor of lobster needs no embellishment.

6 cups cooked lobster meat (about 8 pounds lobster in the
    shell)
¾–1 cup Easy Blender Mayonnaise
1 cup diced chopped celery
Lemon juice (optional)
Salt (optional)
Boston lettuce
3 hard-boiled eggs (optional)

Mix together the lobster, mayonnaise, and celery, reserving the claws. Taste and season with lemon juice and salt if you wish. Mound on leaves of Boston lettuce on a large serving platter. Garnish with wedges of hard-boiled eggs, and top with the reserved claws. (Serves 4 to 6)

VARIATION: *Crabmeat Salad:* Substitute 2 pounds drained crabmeat for the lobster, and add a dash of hot pepper sauce. Omit the eggs and garnish with scored cucumber slices.

Legal's Lobster Meat Casserole

This casserole, which we serve at all our restaurants, is a good choice for company because you can assemble it ahead of time and bake at the last moment. At the restaurants, we moisten the lobster meat with our chowder, but you can use butter or a mixture of fish stock and butter. The lobster should be at room temperature before you bake it, otherwise it will dry out too much.

1/3 cup plus 1 tablespoon butter
1 clove garlic, minced
2 pounds cooked lobster meat, cut into bite-sized pieces
1/2 cup Cracker Crumb Mixture
3/4 cup grated Monterey Jack cheese

Preheat the oven to 400 degrees. Heat the 1/3 cup butter in a saucepan, stir in the garlic, and cook for about 1 minute, stirring constantly. Do not let the butter or garlic brown. Place the lobster in a buttered casserole dish and toss with the melted butter.

Sprinkle the lobster first with the cracker crumbs, and then with the cheese. Dot with the remaining butter. Bake for 12 to 15 minutes, or just until the lobster is heated through and the cheese is melted. Do not overcook or the lobster will toughen and dry out. (Serves 6)

Lobster Sauce for Pasta

The delicate tomato sauce accentuates the flavor of the lobster. Some fish markets give away lobster bodies (or sell them for a minimum sum). If you have the patience to pick the meat, it's an inexpensive way to enjoy lobster.

3 tablespoons olive oil
1½ cups chopped onions
1 teaspoon chopped garlic
4 cups peeled, seeded, and chopped ripe tomatoes
1–1½ cups cooked chopped lobster meat
1 pound fettuccine or spaghetti
1 tablespoon butter

Heat the olive oil in a large casserole, and sauté the onions and garlic for about 10 minutes, or until wilted but not browned. Stir in the tomatoes, lower the heat, and simmer until they reduce slightly and form a sauce, about 15 minutes. Stir the sauce occasionally. Add the lobster meat and cook for only a moment to heat through.

Meanwhile, cook the pasta according to the package directions until it is cooked through but still firm. Drain thoroughly, toss with the butter, then top with the sauce. Serve the pasta immediately. (Serves 4)

VARIATION: *Tomato Crabmeat Sauce for Pasta.* Substitute 8 ounces of crabmeat for the lobster and proceed as above.

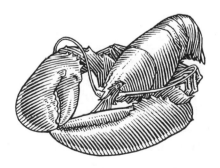

Lobster Milanese

Our son Roger devised this recipe for people who like lobster plain yet tasty. There's no need for drawn butter—although you can serve it with the lobster if you wish. The olive oil keeps the lobster body meat moist, while the claw meat cooks in its own juices.

4 1¼-pound lobsters
4 tablespoons olive oil
4 teaspoons finely minced garlic
Cayenne pepper
4 jumbo shrimp, shelled

Take a lobster, place it stomach side down on the counter, and with a heavy knife cut through the lobster behind the head. This kills the lobster by severing its spine, although it may continue to move after it is dead. Turn the lobster over and cut the body and tail cavities lengthwise down the center.

Gently spread open the lobster's body and brush the cavities with 1 tablespoon of the olive oil. Sprinkle with 1 teaspoon of the garlic and dust with cayenne pepper. Stuff the tail with 1 shrimp and moisten with olive oil.

Repeat this procedure with the remaining lobsters. Place the lobsters on a broiling pan and broil under a preheated broiler for about 8 minutes or until they are cooked through. Do not overcook or the meat will dry out and toughen. (Serves 4)

Mussels

Steamed Mussels

Wash each mussel thoroughly and pull off the "beard" along the side—the dark, hairlike mass the mussel secretes to anchor itself to a rock or other solid object. Some people prefer to add dry white wine rather than water for steaming—either way tastes good. The one essential is a heavy pot. There's no need for salt, because the mussel liquor is salty.

1 large onion, chopped
1/2 cup water
5 pounds mussels, cleaned

Place the onions and water in the bottom of a large, heavy pot. Add the mussels, and immediately bring the water to a boil. Cover the pot, lower the heat slightly, and steam the mussels for 6 to 10 minutes, depending upon their size. Do not overcook, or the mussel flesh will shrivel and lose flavor.

Using a slotted spoon, place the mussels in a serving bowl. Strain the broth through coffee filters and serve with the mussels. (Serves 4)

Mussels au Gratin

This mussel dish, one of the most popular appetizers we serve, also makes an excellent light lunch or supper. We use mussels that are about 2 1/2 inches long for this recipe.

1 cup dry white wine, such as blanc de blancs
5 tablespoons chopped garlic
1 1/2 cups butter (3/4 pound)
1 cup chopped onions
1/2 teaspoon freshly ground pepper
5 pounds cleaned mussels
1 cup chopped parsley leaves
2 cups Cracker Crumb Mixture
2 cups grated Monterey Jack cheese
Lemon wedges
French bread

In a large stainless steel or enameled pot place the wine, 2 tablespoons of the garlic, 1/4 cup of the butter, 1/2 cup of the onions, and the pepper. Bring the mixture to a boil, then add the mussels.

Reduce the heat to medium, cover the pot, and steam the mussels until they open, about 6 to 10 minutes, depending upon their size. Stir the mussels occasionally to redistribute them in the pan. Remove the mussels the moment their shells open because mussels lose flavor if they overcook.

While the mussels are steaming, make the garlic butter. Place 1 cup of the butter in a large mixing bowl and beat it until it is creamy. Mix in the remaining garlic, the remaining onions, and the parsley. Beat this mixture until thoroughly combined, and set aside.

When the mussels are cooked, immediately remove them from the pot with a slotted spoon and break off the top shell. Center each mussel in its shell, and place on a jelly-roll pan or a large baking dish.

Reduce the mussel broth over high heat until the flavor is concentrated and pour it around the mussels in the pan.

Place about 1/2 teaspoon of the garlic butter in each mussel shell. Put the mussels in a preheated 450-degree oven for about 5 minutes, or until the garlic butter melts.

Melt the remaining butter and mix it together with the crumb mixture. Set it aside.

Remove the mussels from the oven and sprinkle with the cheese. Pat the crumb mixture over the mussels, and return them to the oven for about 10 minutes or until the crumb topping is lightly browned.

Serve the mussels immediately, garnished with lemon wedges and accompanied by plenty of French bread to mop up the pan juices. (Serves 4)

Spicy Mussels with Pasta

This is a beautiful dish with the contrasting colors of the blue-black mussels and the deep red of the tomato sauce. Either chorizo or kielbasa works well; which sausage you use depends upon whether you prefer a spicy or a smoky taste.

    4 tablespoons olive oil
    1/2 pound chorizo or kielbasa sausage, sliced into 1/2-inch
      rounds
    1 1/2 cups chopped onions
    4 cups Fresh Tomato Sauce
    1 pound pasta shells or spinach fettuccine
    1 tablespoon butter

3 pounds mussels, cleaned
Salt
Freshly ground pepper

Heat the oil in a large frying pan, add the sausage and 1 cup of the onions, and cook for about 10 minutes, stirring frequently. Add the tomato sauce and simmer, stirring constantly, for 5 minutes longer.

Meanwhile, cook the pasta and steam the mussels. Bring a large pot of water to a boil, add the pasta shells or fettuccine, and cook according to the package directions, about 8 to 15 minutes. Drain the pasta, add 1 tablespoon butter, and keep it warm.

To steam the mussels, place the remaining onions in the bottom of a large, heavy pot along with 1/3 cup water. Add the mussels, and immediately bring the water to a boil. Cover the pot, lower the heat slightly, and steam the mussels for about 6 minutes, or until they open. Do not overcook, or the mussels will lose flavor.

Remove the mussels with a slotted spoon and add to the tomato sauce. Taste the sauce and add salt, pepper, and mussel broth to taste. Place the pasta on a large serving platter and top with the mussels and sauce. Serve immediately. (Serves 4 to 6)

VARIATION: *Spicy Clams with Pasta:* Substitute steamer clams for the mussels.

Oysters

Oyster Stew

This New England oyster stew is simplicity itself. All you need are fresh oysters, butter, milk, and cream—none of which detracts from the flavor of the oysters. The variation includes celery and onions for a change of pace.

> 4 tablespoons butter
> 1½ pound shucked oysters with liquor (about 24)
> 2 cups milk
> 1 cup light cream
> Salt (optional)
> Freshly ground black pepper
> Oyster crackers (optional)

Heat the butter and oysters together in a saucepan until the oysters plump up and the edges begin to curl, between one and two minutes. Meanwhile, in a separate pan, heat the milk and cream together and pour over the oysters. Taste and season with salt and pepper. Serve immediately, accompanied by oyster crackers if you wish. (Serves 4)

VARIATION: *Oyster Stew with Vegetables.* Heat the butter in a large saucepan and add ½ cup chopped onion and ⅓ cup chopped celery or Florence fennel. Stew the vegetables in the butter for about 15 minutes, or until they are soft, then add the oysters and proceed as above. Taste and season with a touch of cayenne pepper or a dash of hot pepper sauce before serving.

Stuffed Oysters

The spinach-and-onion filling sets off the oysters without overpowering their flavor. Oysters vary in their degree of brininess, so taste the oyster liquor before deciding how much liquor to add to the sauce, otherwise the sauce may be too salty.

7 tablespoons butter

1/2 cup chopped scallions, including 2 inches of the green tops

1/2 cup chopped Florence fennel or celery

1 cup chopped onions

1–2 teaspoons chopped garlic

31/2 cups stemmed chopped spinach, tightly packed (about 8 ounces)

2 tablespoons chopped parsley

1 tablespoon minced chives

32 oysters

3 tablespoons flour

1–11/4 cups light cream at room temperature

About 3/4 cup Cracker Crumb Mixture (optional)

3/4–1 cup grated Monterey Jack cheese (optional)

Heat 4 tablespoons of the butter in a large frying pan and add the scallions, fennel, onions, and garlic. Cook slowly, stirring occasionally, letting the vegetables stew in the butter. Do not let the onions brown.

Meanwhile, wash, stem, and chop the spinach. Stir in the spinach and cook, stirring frequently, until it wilts, about 5 minutes. Add the parsley and chives. Set the mixture aside while you make the sauce.

Shuck the oysters, saving the oyster liquor in a measuring cup. Add enough cream to bring the liquid to the 11/4-cup mark. (If the oyster liquor is briny, use only a small amount for flavor.) Or, if you prefer a less concentrated oyster taste, use only the cream. Arrange the oyster halves in two jelly-roll or baking pans.

Heat the remaining butter in a saucepan, remove from the heat, and stir in the flour. Place the mixture over medium heat

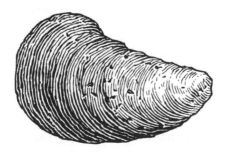

and cook for 2 minutes, stirring constantly. Whisk in the cream, and cook until the sauce thickens.

Purée the spinach mixture in a food processor, add the sauce, and pulse the machine on and off until the mixture is combined.

Place a scant tablespoon of the sauce over each oyster. Sprinkle lightly first with bread crumbs, and then with cheese.

Bake in a preheated 400-degree oven for 18 to 20 minutes or until the oysters are just cooked through, and the cheese has barely turned color. (Serves 6 to 8)

VARIATION: *Mussels with Spinach.* Use 3½ dozen mussels. Steam just until they open, proceed as above, using more crumbs and cheese if necessary. Cook for only 10 to 15 minutes, or just until the cheese melts and lightly browns.

Scallops

Scallops with Basil and Cream

This is a good company dish for nights when you're pressed for time, since it takes less than ten minutes to prepare. This is best with the small Cape scallops. If you are unable to find any, use sea scallops, cut in half.

    4 tablespoons butter
    ¾ cup chopped onions
    1½ teaspoons minced garlic
    2 pounds Cape scallops
    ½ cup dry white wine
    4 tablespoons finely chopped fresh basil leaves
    ½ cup heavy cream
    Salt (optional)

Heat the butter in a large enamel or stainless steel frying pan, add the onions and garlic, and cook for about 5 minutes, or until wilted but not browned.

Add the scallops, and sauté them for about 2 minutes, stirring constantly. Add the wine and continue cooking, stirring constantly, for another 2 minutes. Remove the scallops to a heated platter and set them aside.

Stir in the basil and cream and cook rapidly while the cream reduces and thickens, until it is thick enough to coat a spoon. Taste and season with salt if necessary. Return the scallops to the pan, stir so they are coated with the sauce, and cook for just a minute to reheat them. Do not overcook or they will become rubbery.

Serve immediately with white or brown rice and a garden lettuce salad. (Serves 4)

Scallop and Mushroom Casserole

This is an exceptionally easy dish to make. Only sautéing the mushrooms takes any time. The shrimp variation is a favorite luncheon dish at our restaurants.

    6 tablespoons butter
    1 cup chopped onions
    1 pound mushrooms, sliced
    1 pound scallops
    1/2 cup plus 1 tablespoon Cracker Crumb Mixture
    1/3 cup grated Monterey Jack cheese

Preheat the oven to 450 degrees. Heat 4 tablespoons of the butter in a large frying pan and sauté the onions in it for 2 to 3 minutes, or until they are wilted but not browned. Add the mushrooms and cook, stirring frequently, for about 3 minutes. At this point the mushrooms will have exuded their liquid, and will have dried out. (It's important that this mushroom liquid evaporate, otherwise the completed dish will be watery.)

Spread the mushrooms in the bottom of a large buttered baking dish. Sprinkle with about 1 tablespoon of the Cracker Crumb Mixture. Top with the scallops, then cover with the remaining Cracker Crumb Mixture. Sprinkle the cheese over the cracker crumbs and dot with the remaining 2 tablespoons butter.

Bake the scallops for 15 to 20 minutes or until they are cooked through and the Cracker Crumb Mixture is lightly browned.

Serve with rice. (Serves 4)

VARIATIONS:

Haddock and Mushroom Casserole. Decrease the amount of mushrooms to 3/4 pound. Substitute 1 1/2 pounds haddock fillets for the scallops and sprinkle them with freshly squeezed lemon juice before adding the Cracker Crumb Mixture. Proceed as above. (Serves 4)

Shrimp and Mushroom Casserole. Follow the basic recipe above but decrease the onions to 1/2 cup, add 2 teaspoons chopped garlic, and increase the amount of crumbs to 2/3 cup. Use 1 1/4 pounds shrimp tossed with 2 tablespoons freshly squeezed lime juice. (Serves 4)

Scallop and Onion Stew

The onions enhance the sweet taste of the scallops in this hearty stew.

6–8 tablespoons butter
1 1/2 pounds onions, thinly sliced
1 3/4 pound scallops
4 cups milk
1/2 teaspoon Dijon mustard
Freshly ground pepper
Salt (optional)
1 tablespoon minced parsley or chervil

Heat the butter in a heavy pot, and stir in the onions. Cook them slowly, stirring occasionally, for about 25 minutes, or until they are soft. Add the scallops, and cook for about 3 minutes, stirring constantly.

Pour in the milk, and heat the stew slowly without boiling (otherwise the milk will curdle). Add the mustard.

Taste and add pepper, and salt if you wish. Sprinkle with the fresh herbs.

Serve with crusty French bread. (Serves 4)

VARIATION: *Scallop and Mushroom Stew.* Add ¼ pound mushrooms sautéed in 2 tablespoons of the butter along with the scallops.

Shrimp

Broiled Shrimp with Garlic

Baste the shrimp frequently while they arc broiling so they don't dry out. Ask your fishmonger for shrimp sized about twenty to the pound—shrimp much smaller than that can become tough when broiled.

3/4 cup butter
1/3 cup olive oil
2/3 cup chopped onions
1½ tablespoons minced garlic
3–4 tablespoons freshly squeezed lime juice
A pinch cayenne pepper
2 pounds shrimp, shelled
1/3 cup minced parsley
Salt

Preheat the broiler to 550 degrees. Heat the butter and olive oil together in a large ovenproof pan. Add the onions and garlic and slowly cook them for about 5 minutes, or until softened but not browned.

Stir in the lime juice, cayenne pepper, and shrimp. Continue stirring until the shrimp are coated with the butter mixture.

Broil the shrimp for 5 to 7 minutes, basting once or twice.

Taste and add salt if necessary. Just before serving stir in the parsley. Serve with a good supply of French bread to mop up the juices. (Serves 4)

VARIATIONS:

Broiled Shrimp with Garlic and Tarragon. Stir in 1 1/2 tablespoons chopped fresh tarragon about 2 minutes before the shrimp are done, and reduce the amount of parsley to 2 tablespoons.

Broiled Scallops with Garlic and Lemon. Use only butter or substitute vegetable oil for the olive oil. Substitute 3 tablespoons freshly squeezed lemon juice for the lime juice, and omit the cayenne pepper. The broiling time will vary depending upon the size of the scallops. Bay scallops should be ready in about 5 minutes; the larger sea scallops will take anywhere from 7 to 10 minutes; halve them if you wish.

Shrimp Sautéed with Coriander and Peppers

The pungent taste of the coriander sets off the shrimp. If you prefer, substitute chopped basil or parsley.

4 tablespoons vegetable oil
1 tablespoon minced garlic
1 small onion, minced
3 small green hot peppers, seeded and thinly sliced
1 sweet red pepper, seeded and thinly sliced into 2-inch strips
2 green peppers, seeded and thinly sliced into 2-inch strips
12 scallions, white part only, cut into 1/2-inch lengths
1 1/4 pounds shrimp, shelled
2/3 cup dry white wine
1/2 cup chopped fresh coriander
3–5 tablespoons freshly squeezed lime juice
Freshly ground pepper
Salt

In a large stainless steel or enameled frying pan, heat the oil. Add the garlic, onion, peppers, and scallions. Lower the heat and stir constantly for 3 minutes or until the vegetables are slightly wilted.

Remove the vegetables with a slotted spoon and set them aside. There should be enough oil left in the pan to sauté the shrimp. If not, add another tablespoon of oil. Sauté the shrimp for a minute or until they are almost cooked through.

Add the reserved vegetables, wine, coriander, and lime juice to taste. Stir for a minute, then lower the heat, cover the pan, and cook for 3 to 4 minutes. Taste, season with pepper and salt if necessary and serve over rice. (Serves 4)

Shrimp with Peaches and Peppers

On a summer night when you want something special but don't want to spend much time cooking, try this colorful dish, which takes only about five minutes to cook once the vegetables are prepared. Ripe peaches and freshly squeezed citrus juices are essential for a fresh flavor.

1½ pounds of shrimp, peeled
½ cup freshly squeezed lime juice
2 tablespoons butter
2 tablespoons vegetable or olive oil
1 bunch scallions (about 8), white part only, cut into thin
    rings
2 teaspoons minced garlic
1 large stalk celery, stringed and finely chopped
2 red peppers, seeded and thinly sliced
2 medium tomatoes, peeled, seeded, and coarsely chopped
2 tablespoons chopped basil
3 ripe peaches, peeled and sliced into ¼-inch pieces
¼ cup freshly squeezed orange juice

Marinate the shrimp in the lime juice while you are preparing the vegetables. Heat the butter and oil in a large frying pan and add the scallions. Stir the scallions for about 1 minute, then stir in the garlic and continue cooking for another minute, stirring constantly. Add the celery and red peppers and cook for 1 minute.

Remove the shrimp from the lime-juice marinade, reserving

the juice. Add the shrimp to the vegetable mixture and quickly cook over high heat, stirring constantly. When the shrimp have turned pink (about 1 minute) add the tomato, basil, peaches, and orange juice. Cook for another 2 minutes, then stir in 1/4 cup of the reserved lime juice. (Citrus fruit varies in acidity, so if your oranges are extra sweet, you may wish to add more lime juice.)

Garnish with rings cut from the green part of the scallion before serving. This dish tastes best with rice. (Serves 4)

For a variation, substitute slices of a firm-fleshed fish, such as cusk or monkfish, for the shrimp.

Squid

Squid Stuffed with Scallops and Red Pepper

The contrasting colors of the white squid, topped with a pale coral sauce flecked with red, arranged on a bed of green noodles, makes this an attractive company dish. Don't overcook the squid; the longer it cooks, the more rubbery its texture becomes.

8 tablespoons butter
1 cup chopped onions
2/3 cup diced red pepper
1 teaspoon minced garlic
1/2 pound sea scallops, coarsely chopped
1 1/3 cups bread crumbs, made from densely textured fresh
    white bread
1 tablespoon minced fresh sweet marjoram
Salt
Freshly ground black pepper
A pinch cayenne pepper
1 tablespoon freshly squeezed lime juice
6 medium squid (about 2 pounds) cleaned, washed, and
    dried (see Index for cleaning instructions)
Toothpicks

1/2 cup dry white wine
1 medium tomato, peeled, seeded, and chopped
1 pound spinach fettuccine
1/3 cup heavy cream
Black olives

Heat 4 tablespoons of the butter in a large frying pan and sauté 2/3 cup of the onions and the pepper for about 3 minutes, stirring occasionally. Add the garlic, and sauté 1 minute longer. Stir in the scallops and cook, stirring constantly, for about 2 minutes, or until the scallops have firmed slightly but have not cooked through. Stir in the bread crumbs and marjoram and cook for about 30 seconds, then pour the mixture into a bowl to cool slightly.

Taste the mixture and season with salt, pepper, and the cayenne pepper. Add the lime juice. Loosely stuff the squid with the mixture, remembering that the stuffing will swell and the bodies will shrink as the squid cook. Close the top opening of each squid and fasten with a toothpick.

In a large enameled or stainless steel casserole, heat the remaining butter. Add the wine, tomatoes, and remaining onions and cook for a moment. Top with the squid, cover the pan, and gently stew for about 8 to 10 minutes, turning the squid occasionally in the sauce. Remove from the heat and let the squid sit for about 5 minutes in the covered pan. This allows some of the cooking juices to drain into the sauce, adding flavor.

Meanwhile, cook the fettuccine, and toss with some butter if you wish.

Remove the squid to a dish and quickly boil down the sauce until it thickens. Add the heavy cream and continue to boil until the sauce lightly coats a spoon.

Arrange the fettuccine on a platter and top with the squid arranged in a spoke design. Pour some of the sauce over the squid and garnish with the olives in the center of the dish where the squid meet. Serve with the remaining sauce on the side. (Serves 4 to 6)

Fried Squid with Red Pepper Garlic Sauce

Fried squid is delicious served with this unusual sauce made from grilled red peppers. The sauce goes well with any fried or steamed fish, particularly white-fleshed varieties.

FRIED SQUID
2 pounds squid bodies, cleaned and cut into 1/4-inch rings
Buttermilk, for dipping
A dash hot pepper sauce
About 1 cup Flour Mix for Fried Fish
Vegetable shortening
Red Pepper Garlic Sauce (below)

Cover the squid pieces with buttermilk, add a dash of hot pepper sauce, and let them soak for at least 15 minutes. Shake the excess buttermilk from the squid pieces and toss them in the flour mix. Preheat the vegetable shortening to 365 degrees F. Add the squid, a few pieces at a time, and fry until cooked through, about 1 minute. Serve immediately, accompanied by Red Pepper Garlic Sauce. (Serves 4)

RED PEPPER GARLIC SAUCE
2 large red peppers
1 large egg
4 cloves garlic, peeled and chopped
1/2 teaspoon salt
1/4 teaspoon dry mustard
Hot pepper sauce
2 tablespoons red wine vinegar
1 1/4–1 1/2 cups vegetable oil

Grill or broil the whole red peppers until they are charred on the exterior and cooked through. Place them in a paper bag for 10 minutes, then remove the skin. Cool the peppers and chop them coarsely.

Place the egg and garlic in a blender, and blend until the garlic is puréed. Add the salt, mustard, a dash of hot pepper sauce, the peppers, and the vinegar. Blend until combined. Add 1/4 cup of the oil and pulse the machine on and off for a moment. With the motor running, slowly add the remaining oil. The mixture will thicken to the consistency of a thin mayonnaise. Spoon the sauce into a serving dish and refrigerate until needed. (Makes about 3 cups)

Squid Salad

This perennial favorite at our restaurants has the advantage of keeping well in the refrigerator for several days.

    2 pounds squid, cleaned and cut into 1/2-inch slices
    2 medium carrots, peeled and cut into 1-inch matchstick-
        sized pieces
    2 stalks celery, stringed and cut into 1/2-inch slices
    1 cup chopped red Bermuda onions
    1/2 cup red wine vinegar
    2 cloves garlic, sliced
    1/4 teaspoon dry mustard
    Salt
    Freshly ground black pepper
    1 teaspoon Dijon mustard
    1 1/4 cups olive oil
    2 tablespoons chopped basil or parsley

Drop the squid into a pot of boiling water, and immediately turn off the heat. Let the squid stay in the water for about 1 minute, or until cooked through. Drain the squid and toss with the carrots, celery, and onions in a large bowl.

Meanwhile, combine the vinegar, garlic, dry mustard, salt, and pepper. Let the mixture sit for about 30 minutes to meld the flavors. Add the Dijon mustard and olive oil, and whisk to combine. Heat the vinaigrette sauce until almost boiling, remove the garlic, and pour over the squid. Toss with the basil. Press down slightly on the mixture so it is submerged in the marinade. Let the squid marinate for at least 4 hours. Before serving, drain off the excess marinade. (Serves 4 to 6)

VARIATION: Add 2 roasted, peeled, and chopped red peppers to the vegetable mixture.

A Mélange
of Soups, Salads,
and Basic Recipes

This chapter includes some of my favorite recipes, such as our Inaugural Fish Chowder and our Onion Strings, which don't fit into any other spot in the book. You can turn almost any salad into a main-course version by adding leftover sliced fish, but the salads you'll find here are something special. If you've never made tartar sauce, I think you'll find that Legal's version is well worth the small amount of time it takes to assemble the ingredients. Our unusual Fish Stock contains grated carrots which add a subtle sweetness that many people enjoy.

You'll discover how to make a home version of the corn-flour mix we use to coat our fried foods as well as a cracker-crumb fish topping that keeps for weeks when refrigerated.

I've also included a few desserts, such as the old-fashioned Grape-Nuts Custard that's a favorite with our customers.

Inaugural Fish Chowder

We made hundreds of gallons of this chowder for a gala event featuring the food of selected restaurants from around the country for the 1981 Presidential Inaugural in Washington. People say they've never had chowder as flavorful as ours. Its unique taste derives from a concentrated Fish Stock made from the fish frames remaining from the white-fleshed fish we fillet as well as a generous mixture of white-fleshed fish such as cod and monkfish. This chowder recipe is delicious, but it will never taste quite the same as Legal's because you can't approximate the concentrated fish base at home. The chowder tastes best if you prepare it a few hours in advance to allow the flavors to meld.

1/2 cup butter
3 cups diced onions
1/4 cup finely grated carrots
2 teaspoons minced garlic
1/2 cup flour
12 cups concentrated Fish Stock
4 pounds chowder fish fillets, such as 2 pounds cod, 1
    pound monkfish, and 1 pound cusk
2 cups light cream
1/2 cup finely grated Monterey Jack cheese
Salt
Freshly ground black pepper

Heat the butter in a large saucepan until softened, and sauté the onions, carrots, and garlic in it, stirring frequently, about 5 minutes. Remove from heat and slowly stir in the flour. Return to the heat, and cook, stirring, for about 4 minutes. Meanwhile, begin heating the stock in a large pot. Whisk the stock into the flour mixture. Bring the stock to a boil, whisking constantly, then reduce the heat, and simmer for 10 minutes.

Add the fish and simmer about 10 minutes longer. Stir in the cream and cheese, and simmer until the cheese melts, about 5 to 8 minutes. (You won't distinguish the cheese as such, it is incorporated into the chowder.) Reheat the chowder slowly so the cream doesn't boil. (Makes about 3 quarts)

Seafood and Pasta Salad

Most seafood and pasta salads have an abundance of pasta and a dearth of seafood. Our salad is chock-full of seafood with the pasta serving merely as a textural and color contrast. We like it that way, but if you prefer a more traditional salad, increase the amount of pasta. It's important to use not only a good-quality olive oil but also a fine red wine vinegar such as the Chianti vinegar we import from Italy, which adds an extra flavor dimension to the salad.

    1 pound spinach tortellini stuffed with cheese
    4–6 ounces pasta shells
    1 pound cleaned squid
    1 pound peeled, cleaned shrimp
    1/4 pound smoked mussels
    1/4 pound pitted black olives
    1/2 pound Marinated Mushrooms
    3/4 cup julienned sun-dried tomatoes (about 1 1/2 ounces)
    1 clove garlic, minced
    1/2 cup virgin olive oil
    1/3 cup red wine vinegar
    Salt
    Freshly ground pepper

Bring a large pot of water to a boil, add the tortellini and boil until cooked through but not soft. Drain thoroughly and place the pasta in a large bowl.

Repeat the cooking procedure for the pasta shells, drain them, and add to the bowl.

Slice the squid bodies into 1/4-inch pieces, leaving the tentacles whole. Bring a pot of water to a boil, add the squid and gently boil until the squid is barely cooked through, about 1 minute. Do not overcook or the squid will have the texture of rubber bands. Drain the squid and add to the bowl.

Steam and drain the shrimp and add them to the bowl. Stir in the mussels, olives, mushrooms, and tomatoes and toss thoroughly.

Thoroughly combine the garlic, olive oil, and vinegar, preferably in a food processor so the mixture is emulsified and won't separate. Toss with the salad. There is enough dressing to coat the ingredients without drowning them in a pool of oil and vinegar. Taste and season with salt and pepper. (Serves 8)

Two-toned Fettuccine with Seafood

This colorful pasta dish, subtly flavored with saffron, is an excellent choice for a special dinner. Use fresh basil rather than dried, because the basil oils contribute to the flavor of the finished dish.

    1/8 teaspoon fine-quality saffron
    1 tablespoon boiling water
    16 mussels (about 1 1/4 pounds), cleaned
    1/2 pound scallops
    1/2 pound haddock or cusk
    8 ounces egg fettuccine
    8 ounces spinach fettuccine
    4 tablespoons butter
    1/3 cup minced onions
    1–2 cloves garlic, minced
    1/2 medium carrot, julienned into matchstick-sized pieces
    1/2 medium zucchini, julienned into matchstick-sized pieces
    1 large tomato, peeled, seeded, and coarsely chopped
    1/3 cup heavy cream
    3 tablespoons minced basil
    2 tablespoons minced chives
    Salt
    Freshly ground black pepper

Crumble the saffron threads between your fingers, place them in a bowl, and cover with the boiling water. Let steep while you prepare the pasta sauce.

Steam the mussels in a large pot along with 1/4 cup water. When the mussels have opened, remove them from their shells, reserving any liquid in the pot. Place the mussel meat in a large bowl.

Place 1 inch of water in the bottom of a steamer, and steam the scallops and haddock until they are just cooked through. Remove from the steamer, reserving any cooking juices at the bottom of the pot. Thinly slice the scallops and flake the haddock into the bowl containing the mussels. Reduce the cooking juices by boiling to concentrate the flavor, and add to the mussel liquid. Measure out the mussel and scallop liquid. You should have about 1 cup. If you have more, boil it until it is reduced to 1 cup. Set the liquid aside.

Cook the fettuccine in a large pot of boiling water. (If it is fresh fettuccine, boil it after the sauce is done, because it will take only a couple of minutes to cook.)

While the fettuccine is boiling, heat 3 tablespoons of the butter in a large frying pan and sauté the onions and garlic for 2 minutes. Add the carrots and zucchini and cook the vegetables for 1 minute longer, stirring constantly. Stir in the tomatoes and cook another minute. Add the reserved saffron liquid and the seafood liquid to the pot containing the vegetables. Cover it and simmer for about 3 minutes. Do not overcook the vegetables; they should still be slightly crisp. Remove the vegetables with a slotted spoon and place them in the bowl with the seafood.

The seafood liquid forms the base of the sauce, so it is important that it be as flavorful as possible. Reduce the sauce to about 2/3 cup. Add the cream and simmer for another minute to amalgamate the flavors. Stir in the seafood and vegetables and reheat them. Add the basil and chives. Taste the sauce and season with salt and pepper if necessary.

Thoroughly drain the fettuccine, toss with the remaining butter, and top with the sauce. Serve immediately. (Serves 6 to 8)

VARIATION: Substitute rotini, penne, or shells for the fettuccine, and shrimps for the scallops.

Warm Shellfish Salad

This delicious company dish, suitable for a spring evening, is best served warm.

1 1½-pound lobster
1 pound mussels (about ¼ pound), shelled and cooked
1 onion, chopped
¾ pound sea scallops
½ pound shelled shrimp
2 tablespoons butter
2 ounces good-quality diced country ham
¼ cup vegetable oil
2 tablespoons mild vinegar
Chinese sesame oil
1 teaspoon Dijon mustard
2–3 tablespoons cooked mussel or scallop pan broth
1 teaspoon minced chives
1 head washed and dried chicory

Steam or boil the lobster until cooked through, and set aside. Steam the mussels and onions along with enough water to cover the bottom of the pan until the mussels have opened, about 8 minutes. Set them aside, reserving the pan broth.

Steam the scallops and shrimp together in a steamer with enough water to cover the bottom of the pan. Place them in a bowl, reserving the pan broth.

Meanwhile, heat the butter in a medium-sized fry pan and sauté the ham in it until it is cooked through and barely browned. Remove the ham from the fat with a slotted spoon and add to the bowl containing the scallops and shrimp, and toss.

Remove the mussels from their shells and toss with the ham, scallops and shrimp.

Remove the lobster meat from the tail, slice it thin, and add it to the shellfish mixture. Remove the lobster tomalley from the body cavity and place it in a large mixing bowl. (Set the remaining lobster aside for a sandwich or, if you prefer, add the meat from the entire lobster to the salad.)

To the mixing bowl containing the tomalley, add the vegetable oil, vinegar, a drop or two of sesame oil, the mustard, 2–3 tablespoons of the shellfish pan broth, and the chives. Pour this dressing over the shellfish and mix thoroughly. Taste and add more sesame oil or shellfish broth if you prefer.

Serve warm over crisp chicory leaves. (Serves 4 to 6)

Seafood Salad

This is an excellent salad for times when you don't feel like cooking. It will keep for a few days in the refrigerator, provided the seafood is immersed in the sauce in a tightly covered dish.

    1/3 cup dry white wine
    1/2 onion, chopped
    1 clove garlic, chopped
    1 1/2 pounds mussels, cleaned
    1 pound monkfish
    1 pound scallops
    1/4 pound shrimp
    1/3 cup lemon juice
    Minced rind of 1 lemon
    1/2 cup vegetable oil
    1/2 teaspoon sesame oil
    1 large red pepper, seeded and cut into matchstick-sized
        pieces about 1 inch long
    1 tablespoon chopped fresh sweet marjoram
    5 scallions, white parts only, chopped
    1/4 cup liquid from steamed fish
    Pinch of dry mustard
    Pinch of salt

Place the wine, onions, garlic, and mussels in a large pot, bring the liquid to a boil, lower the heat, and steam the mussels until they just open, about 5 to 8 minutes, depending upon their size. Remove the mussels from the pot, reserving the mussel liquor. Set the mussels aside.

Strain the mussel liquor and place it in the bottom of a steamer, adding water if necessary. Steam the monkfish, scallops, and shrimp, removing each type of seafood as it is done. Save the liquid in the bottom of the pot.

Remove the mussels from their shells, slice the monkfish and scallops into 1/4-inch pieces, and slice the shrimp if you wish.

Mix together the lemon juice, lemon rind, vegetable oil, sesame oil, red peppers, sweet marjoram, scallions, and 1/4 cup of the reserved liquid exuded by the fish. Taste and season with the mustard and salt, and additional fish liquor, if necessary.

Toss the dressing with the fish and let sit for at least 1 hour before serving, to allow the flavors to meld. (Serves 4)

Fish Cakes

Fish cakes made with salted codfish were standard New England fare for generations. This version uses cooked fresh fish for cakes that make a good breakfast dish or a light Sunday supper. Handle them gently, and use freshly mashed potatoes for best results.

6 tablespoons butter
1/3 cup chopped scallions, white parts only
1 2/3 cups freshly mashed potatoes
1 tablespoon sour cream
6 ounces flaked cooked white-fleshed fish, such as cod, haddock, pollock, halibut, or flounder
1 egg
1/4 teaspoon dry mustard
Salt
Freshly ground black pepper
3 tablespoons minced parsley
Dried bread crumbs
1 tablespoon olive or vegetable oil

Heat 2 tablespoons of the butter and sauté the scallions in it for about 5 minutes, stirring frequently. Do not allow the scallions to brown. Set them aside.

Meanwhile, cook the potatoes, and when they are soft, drain, and mash them with 1 tablespoon of the butter and the sour cream. Combine them with the fish and set aside.

Beat the egg, and add the mustard, a generous amount of salt, and black pepper. Stir in the scallions and parsley. Combine this mixture with the potatoes and fish. (I find a spatula works best. Do not use a mixer, or the potatoes will become gummy.)

Form the codfish mixture into 8 cakes about 2½ inches in diameter and dip each cake into the bread crumbs. Heat the remaining butter and the oil in a large frying pan, and sauté the codfish cakes slowly for about 3 minutes on each side, or until they are lightly browned and cooked through. Serve with catsup on the side. (Serves 4)

VARIATION: *Fresh Salmon and Dill Cakes.* Substitute 8 ounces flaked cooked salmon for the white-fleshed fish, and 2 table-spoons minced fresh dill and 1 tablespoon minced parsley for the 3 tablespoons parsley. Use either dried bread crumbs or crushed cracker crumbs. Proceed as above. For a savory version, add a dash of Worchestershire sauce and hot pepper sauce along with the dill.

Marinated Mushrooms

These mushrooms are delicious served alone as an appetizer or as an ingredient in Seafood and Pasta Salad.

    2 pounds mushrooms
    2 cups red wine vinegar
    8 ounces finely diced onions
    1 ounce pickling spices, tied up in cheesecloth
    8 ounces diced pimentos
    4 ounces good quality olive oil
    Salt
    Freshly ground black pepper

Clean the mushrooms and blanch them in a pot of boiling water for 30 seconds. Drain them and set aside.

Bring the vinegar to a boil in an cnameled or stainless steel pan. Add the onions and pickling spices, turn the heat to sim-mer, and cook for 2 minutes. Add the mushrooms to the vine-gar, along with the pimentos, olive oil, salt, and pepper to taste. Cool the mixture and store in the refrigerator, where the mush-rooms will stay in good condition for at least 2 weeks. (Makes 2 pounds)

Onion Strings

These are more delicate-tasting than onion rings, which accounts for much of their popularity at our restaurants. The trick is to cut the onions as thin as possible, and to soak them for a few minutes in buttermilk before frying.

2 pounds large yellow onions
4 cups buttermilk
3 pounds vegetable shortening
3–4 cups Flour Mix for Fried Fish

Peel the onions. Cut out a wedge from the top to the bottom of each onion.

Place an onion sideways on the counter, and hold it tightly with one hand, almost squeezing the onion closed. (This makes it easier to cut thin slices.) Slice the onion as thin as possible, and separate each strand. Continue this process until all the onions are sliced.

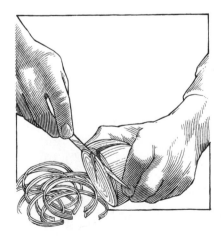

Cover the onions with buttermilk and soak for at least 15 minutes. Meanwhile, heat the shortening to 360 degrees. Drain the onion slices and toss them in the flour mixture.

Place a small batch of onion strings in the heated fat and deep-fry until they are lightly browned and crisp. This will take about 30 seconds per batch. Continue frying the onions until all the strings are cooked. Drain the onion strings on paper towels, and serve immediately. (Serves 4)

Cocktail Sauce

This is the traditional dipping sauce to accompany shrimp cocktail.

1/2 cup chili sauce
1/4 cup catsup
2 tablespoons freshly squeezed lemon juice
5 teaspoons bottled grated horseradish
Hot pepper sauce
1/4 teaspoon Worcestershire sauce

Mix together the chili sauce, catsup, lemon juice, horseradish, a dash of hot pepper sauce, and Worcestershire sauce. Store any leftover sauce in a covered jar in the refrigerator where it will keep for at least two weeks. (Makes about 1 cup)

Fish Stock

Our fish stock includes a carrot, which adds a mellow flavor.

6 pounds fish frames, with gills and intestines removed
1 stalk celery
1 carrot, sliced
2 onions, sliced
4 peppercorns

Chop the fish into pieces. Place the pieces in a large enameled or stainless steel casserole along with the celery, carrot, onions, and peppercorns. Cover with 3 quarts water. Bring the water to a boil, lower the heat, and simmer for about 30 minutes.

Strain off the stock and boil it 25 to 30 minutes to concentrate the flavor. If you wish, clarify by pouring through coffee filters before storing.

Measure the stock into 1-cup amounts, and freeze. (Makes about 8 cups)

Fresh Tomato Sauce

Use this sauce with Fish Parmigiana or toss it with leftover fish and pasta. Any extra sauce will keep in the refrigerator for up to a week or in the freezer for three months. Watch the cooking time, because the longer tomatoes cook, the more acidic they become.

> 1/4 cup olive oil
> 2 cups chopped onions
> 1/4 cup grated carrot
> 1 teaspoon minced garlic
> 5 cups peeled, seeded, and chopped tomatoes
> 1 tablespoon chopped sweet marjoram or oregano
> 2 tablespoons chopped basil
> Salt (optional)

Heat the oil in a large enameled or stainless steel saucepan. Add the onions, carrot, and garlic. Cook, stirring frequently, until the vegetables are cooked through but have not browned. Add the tomatoes. Partially cover the pan, and simmer for 15 minutes. Sieve the sauce or lightly process in a food processor. Pour the sauce back into the pan and add the marjoram and basil. Partially cover and simmer for 10 minutes longer. Taste and season with salt if necessary. (Makes about 4 cups)

Coleslaw

This remains the most popular accompaniment to fried fish.

> 5 cups shredded green cabbage
> 3 cups shredded red cabbage
> 1 medium onion, peeled and shredded
> 1 1/2 cups shredded carrots

1–1 1/4 cups mayonnaise
3/4 cup sour cream, or 1/2 cup sour cream and 1/2 cup
   yogurt
Salt

Pour boiling water over the green cabbage and let sit for 5
minutes. Drain and press dry. Toss with the red cabbage, onions, and carrots.

Add the mayonnaise and sour cream. Salt to taste and add
additional mayonnaise if you like. (Serves 6 to 8)

VARIATIONS:
Substitute Florence fennel for the red cabbage. Add celery or
anise seeds to taste. Add 1/4 cup chopped red or green pepper.

Tartar Sauce

Serve this sauce with fried seafood, or use it instead of mayonnaise in a fish sandwich. As you can see, our sauce gets its flavor
from a number of ingredients, most of which you probably have
on hand. This is one case where commercial mayonnaise works
well because it has a heavier texture than a homemade version.

1 cup mayonnaise
2 tablespoons minced onions
2 tablespoons finely chopped kosher dill pickles
2 tablespoons finely chopped mixed sweet pickles
1/4 teaspoon juice from sweet pickles
1 tablespoon minced celery
1 tablespoon minced green pepper
1 teaspoon minced garlic
1 teaspoon sweet pepper relish
1 teaspoon sweet red pepper relish
Hot pepper sauce
1/4 teaspoon white vinegar
1/4 teaspoon dry mustard
1/2–1 teaspoon freshly squeezed lemon juice
1 teaspoon Dijon mustard, preferably country style

Combine the mayonnaise, onions, pickles, juice, celery, green
pepper,

garlic, relishes, a dash of hot pepper sauce, vinegar, dry mustard, lemon juice to taste, and Dijon mustard. Let the flavors meld for an hour or two before serving. Any extra sauce keeps for at least a week in the refrigerator if stored in a covered container. (Makes about 1 1/4 cups)

Flour Mix for Fried Fish

Corn flour, available at many fish and health food stores, gives a finer texture than cornmeal, but you can approximate the same results by whirling cornmeal in a food processor.

1 1/2 cups yellow corn flour or cornmeal
2 cups flour
1/2 teaspoon dry mustard
1 teaspoon salt
1/8 teaspoon cayenne pepper

If using cornmeal, whirl it in a food processor for about 1 minute. Add the flour, dry mustard, salt, and cayenne pepper, and pulse the machine on and off a few times to mix the ingredients. Store the mixture in a covered glass jar on the pantry shelf. (Makes about 3 1/2 cups)

VARIATION: For a spicer version, add 1/2 teaspoon black pepper and 1/2 teaspoon garlic powder along with the flour and spices.

Cracker Crumb Mixture

This rich crumb topping keeps well on the pantry shelf or in the refrigerator. Halve the recipe if you use crumbs sparingly.

1 1/2 pounds oyster crackers
1/4 cup finely chopped onions
2 cups clarified butter (about 1 1/2 pounds butter)
1/4 cup minced parsley
2 teaspoons dried thyme or herbes de Provence

Whirl the crackers in a food processor or put them through a food grinder until they are evenly ground but retain some texture. Sauté the onions in 2 tablespoons of the butter, then add to the crumb mixture along with the remaining butter, parsley, and thyme. Mix thoroughly. If the mixture hardens in the refrigerator, place it in the oven on low heat for a few minutes before using. (Makes about 9 cups)

Easy Blender Mayonnaise

Use this mayonnaise for crabmeat or lobster rolls; as a base for an herb mayonnaise to serve with salmon or striped bass; or spread it on scrod and bake with cracker crumbs.

1 large egg
2 tablespoons cider or malt vinegar
1/2 teaspoon dry mustard
1/2 teaspoon salt
1 cup vegetable oil

In a blender container put the egg, vinegar, mustard, salt, and 1/4 cup of the vegetable oil. Turn on the motor and immediately pour in the rest of the oil in a slow, steady stream. The mixture will thicken as the oil is poured in.

Store the mayonnaise in a covered jar in the refrigerator where it will keep for about 3 weeks. (Makes about 1 cup)

VARIATIONS:

Garlic Mayonnaise. This is delicious served with poached fish or stirred into a thick fish soup. Add 3 chopped garlic cloves (about 1 tablespoon) along with the egg, and proceed as above.

Walnut Garlic Mayonnaise. Try this instead of tartar sauce with fried fish. Be sure to let the mayonnaise sit for a day or two before serving to allow the flavors time to meld. Blend together 1/2 cup walnuts and 1 tablespoon chopped garlic. Set the mixture aside. Make mayonnaise as above. Just before the mayonnaise is finished, add the walnut mixture and pulse three or four times to incorporate. Do not overmix or the mayonnaise will separate.

Fresh Applesauce

We serve this applesauce over gingerbread as a dessert at our restaurants. The long, slow cooking produces a flavorful sauce, while the apple skins add both flavor and color.

5 pounds McIntosh apples, stemmed and cut into chunks
1/3 cup water
1 cup sugar
1/3 cup freshly squeezed lemon juice
2 teaspoons cinnamon

Place the apples and water in a large stainless steel or enameled pot, cover, and steam for about 10 minutes, stirring frequently. Add the sugar, lemon juice, and cinnamon, partially cover the pot, and continue to cook slowly for about 1½ hours. Stir the mixture often, and add more water if necessary.

Put the apple mixture through a food mill to remove the skins and seeds, then chill. Serve over Gingerbread. (Makes about 8 cups)

Gingerbread

This densely textured gingerbread is one of the favorite desserts at our restaurants. We serve it topped with Fresh Applesauce.

1/4 cup butter
1/3 cup vegetable shortening
2/3 cup sugar
2 eggs
3/4 cup molasses
4 cups flour
1½ teaspoons ginger
3/4 teaspoon cinnamon
1/2 teaspoon ground cloves
2 teaspoons baking soda
1/2 teaspoon salt
2 cups plus 2 tablespoons buttermilk

Preheat the oven to 375 degrees. Cream the butter and shortening together. Add the sugar and continue beating until the mixture increases in volume, about 5 minutes. Beat in the eggs, one at a time. Add the molasses.

Sift together the flour, ginger, cinnamon, cloves, baking soda, and salt. Add the flour mixture to the batter alternately with the buttermilk.

Pour the batter into a buttered 13 × 9-inch baking pan. Bake for about 40 minutes, or until a knife inserted into the center comes out clean. Cool the gingerbread in the pan before cutting into serving pieces. (Makes a 13 × 9-inch loaf)

Grape-Nut Custard

This custard appeals to hearty appetites. At the restaurants we serve man-sized portions topped with whipped cream. It's worth buying a nutmeg grater and whole nutmegs, because freshly grated nutmeg adds a delicious flavor and aroma to the completed dish never equaled by packaged nutmeg.

    10 eggs
    1 cup sugar
    4½ cups milk
    Pinch of salt
    1 teaspoon vanilla
    ½–⅔ cup Grape-Nuts cereal
    Nutmeg
    Whipped cream (optional)

Preheat the oven to 325 degrees. Beat the eggs until combined, then beat in the sugar. Continue beating until the eggs increase in volume and the color of the mixture lightens, about 2 to 3 minutes.

Meanwhile, heat the milk to just below the boiling point, and also boil a large kettle of water.

Stir the hot milk into the eggs, then beat in the salt and vanilla. Sprinkle the Grape-Nuts over the bottom of a large 3-quart baking pan. Strain the custard mixture through a fine sieve into the baking pan. (Omit this step if you wish, but it removes any stringy parts of the egg whites.) Sprinkle grated nutmeg over the top.

Place the baking pan into a large, deep roasting pan, such as a turkey roaster, and pour the boiling water halfway up the sides of the baking pan. Place on the lowest shelf of the oven. Bake for 50 to 55 minutes, or until a knife inserted in the center comes out clean. Start checking after 45 minutes, because if you over-cook the custard it develops little bubbles on the bottom and a slightly grainy texture.

Cool before serving with whipped cream on top. The custard will keep for about a week in the refrigerator if covered with plastic wrap or foil. (Serves 6–10)

INDEX

Anchovies, in Mackerel or Tuna Salad Niçoise, 72–73
Aphrodisiac, oysters as, 117
Applesauce, 172
Asparagus, Halibut with, 70–71

Bacon
  in Monkfish Baked with Herbs and Mustard, 76
  Shad Roe with, 87
    and Mushrooms and Tomatoes, 87
Bacteria, 18, 19
Baked Flounder with Ham and Olive Butter, 68
Baked Monkfish with Herbs and Mustard, 76
Baked Salmon with Mint or Dill, 59
Baked Scrod. See Scrod—Baked
Baked Sea Bass with Herbs, 58–59
Baked Sole, Easy, 89
Baking, 41–42
Barbecuing, 23

Basil
  in Broiled Tuna with Salsa, 98
  in Grilled Mackerel with Garlic Mayonnaise, 73
  Grilled Striped Bass with Garlic and, 59
  in Monkfish Baked with Herbs and Mustard, 76
  Scallops with, and Cream, 144–45
  in Swordfish with Tomatoes and Mussels, 95
Bass, 58–59
  general characteristics of, 24–25
  Sea, Baked, with Herbs, 58–59
  Striped, Grilled, with Garlic and Basil, 59
Blood clots, reducing formation of, 25, 29
Bluefin tuna, 12
Bluefish, 12, 60–63
  with Citrus Juices, 62–63
  distinctive flavor of, 24
  general characteristics of, 25–26

marination of, 23
with Mustard Sauce, 61–62
Smoked, Pâté, 60–61
Braising, 23
Breaded Sole with Herbs, 90
Brined fish, 18
Broccoli, Halibut with, 71
Broiled Coho Salmon with a Chive
Butter Sauce, 81–82
Broiled Flounder with Olive Butter, 67
Broiled Haddock, 43
Broiled Scallops with Garlic and Lemon,
148
Broiled Shrimp with Garlic, 147–48
and Tarragon, 148
Broiled Swordfish with Salsa, 97–98
Broiled Tuna with Salsa, 98
Broiling, 42–43
Butter
Browned, Sole with, 67
Chive Sauce, Broiled Coho Salmon
with, 81–82
drawn, description of, 135
Garlic-Parsley, Steamed Clams with,
130–31
Olive, Baked Flounder with Ham and,
68
Olive, Broiled Flounder with, 67
Sole with Herbs and, 67

Calcium, 13
Calories in a serving of fish, 12
Capers, Sauce of Lemon Juice and,
Fresh Tuna in, 99
Casseroles
Haddock and Mushroom, 146
Legal's Lobster Meat Casserole, 136
Scallop and Mushroom, 145–46
Shrimp and Mushroom, 146
Child, Julia, 6–7
Chilled Salmon and Cucumber Soup, 79
Chives
Butter Sauce, Broiled Coho Salmon
with, 81–82
Sautéed Shad Roe with, and Lemon,
87–88
Cholesterol, 25, 106
Chowder
Clam, 129–30
Inaugural Fish, 158
Citrus Juices
Bluefish with, 62–63

Scrod with, 63
Clambake, 106–7
Clams, 106, 129–31
cherrystone, 107
Chowder, 129–30
cleaning of, 108
cooking time for, 40
Fried, 45
general characteristics of, 106–8
hard-shell, 107, 108
littleneck, 107
soft-shell, 107, 108
Spicy, with Pasta, 141
Steamed, with Garlic-Parsley Butter,
130–31
Cleanliness, 19–20
Cod, 40
already butchered on the boats, 19
Broiled, with Bread or Cracker
Crumbs, 43
Fish Cakes, 164–65
general characteristics of, 26
Parmigiana, 100–1
Soup, 63–64
Steamed, with Vegetables, 49–50
Coleslaw, 168–69
Connective tissue, fish compared to
meat, 11, 39–40
Cooking techniques, 37–54
Cooking time for fish, 40–41
shellfish, 105
lobsters, 134–35, 138
squid, 123
steaming, 50
See also Overcooking
Coriander
in Broiled Swordfish with Salsa, 97–98
Sauce, Sweet and Sour, Salmon with,
80
Shrimp Sautéed with Peppers and,
148–49
Corn, Pollock with, and Zucchini and
Peppers, 77
Crabmeat, 108–9
imitation, 110
Roll, 132
Salad, 136
Sauce
Pasta with, 134
Tomato, for Pasta, 137
Sole Stuffed with, 90–91
with Tomatoes, 133

Crabs, 106, 131–34
    Alaskan king, 109–10, 132
    Deviled, 132–33
    Dungeness, 110
    general characteristics of, 108–10
    soft-shell
        cleaning, 109
        Fried, 45
        Sautéed, 131
    stone, 109
    See also Crabmeat
Cracker Crumb Mixture, 170–71
Cream cheese, in Smoked Bluefish Pâté,
        60–61
Cucumbers
    Garnish, Grilled Tuna with, 98
    Soup, with Chilled Salmon, 79
Cusk
    in a Fresh Tomato Sauce, 69–70
    general characteristics of, 26–27
    Parmigiana, 100–1
    Savory, 85
    Spicy Fried, with Guacamole Sauce,
        64–65
    as stew fish, 23
Custard, Grape-Nut, 173–74
Cutting the fish, 51–52

Dabs, 27, 33
Desserts, 172–74
Dill
    Cakes, Fresh Salmon, 165
    Salmon Baked with, 59
Drawn butter, description of, 135

Easy Blender Mayonnaise, 171
Eels, 12

Farmed salmon, 30–31
Fats in fish, compared to meat and
        cheese, 11–12
Fatty fish, 12
Fettucine
    in Squid Stuffed with Scallops and
        Red Pepper, 150–51
    Two-toned, with Seafood, 160–61
Filleting the fish, 52–54
Fillets, fresh vs. old, 18
Fish Cakes, 164–65
Fish diet, healthiness of, 11–13
Fish Stock, 167–68
Flatfish, 40

Flounder, 19, 23, 28, 33, 66–68
    Baked, with Ham and Olive Butter, 68
    Broiled, with Olive Butter, 68
    in Europe, 13
    Fish Cakes, 164–65
    general characteristics of, 27
    iodine aftertaste from, 122
    Sautéed, 48–49
    Stuffed
        with Salmon, 67
        with Smoked Salmon, 67
        with Vegetables, 66–67
Flour Mix for Fried Fish, 170
Flukes, 27, 33
Fresh Applesauce, 172
Fresh fish, 17–19, 57
    fatty fish vs. leaner fish, 28
    lobsters, 112
    mussels, 115–16
    oysters, 106, 117
    pollock, 30
    scallops, 120
    shrimp, 122–23
    squid, 123
Fresh Salmon and Dill Cakes, 165
Fresh Tomato Sauce, 168
Fried Clams, 45
Fried fish
    Coleslaw with, 168–69
    Flour Mix for, 170
    Tartar Sauce for, 169–70
Fried Oysters, 45
Fried Pollock, 44–45
Fried Shrimp, 45
Fried Soft-Shell Clams, 45
Fried Squid with Red Pepper Garlic
        Sauce, 152–53
Frozen fish, 41
    shrimp, 121, 122
Frying, 43–45

Garlic
    Broiled Scallops with Lemon and, 148
    Broiled Shrimp with, 147–48
        and Tarragon, 148
    Grilled Striped Bass with, and Basil,
        59
    Mayonnaise, 171
        Grilled Mackerel with, 73
    -Parsley Butter, Steamed Clams with,
        130–31

-Red Pepper Sauce, Fried Squid with,
    152–53
Gingerbread, 172–73
Goat cheese, in Pollock with Corn,
    Zucchini, and Peppers, 78
Grapefruit, in Salmon with a Sweet and
    Sour Coriander Sauce, 80
Grape-Nut Custard, 173–74
Gray sole, 27, 33
Green beans, in Monkfish, Bean, and
    Pepper Salad, 75–76
Grilled Halibut, 46
Grilled Mackerel with Garlic
    Mayonnaise, 73
Grilled Striped Bass with Garlic and
    Basil, 59
Grilled Swordfish with Orange Sauce,
    96–97
Grilled Tuna with a Cucumber Garnish,
    98
Grilling, 45–46
Guacamole Sauce
    Fried Shrimp with, 65
    Spicy Fried Cusk with, 64–65

Haddock, 19
    Broiled, 43
    Casserole, with Mushrooms, 146
    conservation measures for, 13
    Fish Cakes, 164–65
    in a Fresh Tomato Sauce, 69–70
    general characteristics of, 27–28
    lack of fat in, 11–12
    Parmigiana, 100–1
    as stew fish, 23
Halibut, 23, 70–71
    with Asparagus, 70–71
    with Broccoli, 71
    delicate flavor of, 24
    Fish Cakes, 164–65
    general characteristics of, 28
    Grilled, 46
    Parmigiana, 100–1
    Savory, 85
    with Watercress Sauce, 71
Ham, Baked Flounder with, and Olive
    Butter, 68
Heart disease, 12, 29
Herb Cheese, Scrod Baked with, and
    Crumbs, 86
Herbs, 57
    Baked Sea Bass with, 58–59

Breaded Sole with, 90
Monkfish Baked with, and Mustard, 76
Sole with, and Butter, 49

Inaugural Fish Chowder, 158
Incidental catch, definition of, 30
Iodine aftertaste, 122–23

Kabobs
    Scallop, 94–95
    Swordfish, 94
Kelley, Vicki, v

Legal's Lobster Meat Casserole, 136
Legal Sea Foods
    buying of fish at, 5, 19
    history of, 3–8
    immediate serving of fish at, 6, 40
    processing of fish at, 19–20
Lemon juice
    in Broiled Scallops with Garlic and
        Lemon, 148
    Fresh Tuna in Sauce of Capers and,
        99
    Sautéed Shad Roe with, and Chives,
        87–88
Lemon sole, 27, 33
Lime Juice, Tuna with, 99
Lobster, 106, 134–38
    Boiled, 134–35
    general characteristics of, 110–12
    how to eat, 112–14
    Legal's Lobster Meat Casserole, 136
    Milanese, 138
    poor man's, 29
    Salad, 135–36
    Sauce for Pasta, 137
    size and weight of, 111
        cooking time for boiled lobster,
            134–35
    in Warm Shellfish Salad, 162–63
Lotte, 29

Mackerel, 12, 23, 72–74
    general characteristics of, 28–29
    Grilled, with Garlic Mayonnaise, 73
    Marinated, 74
    Niçoise, 72
    with Red Peppers and Onions, 74
Marinated Mackerel, 74
Marinated Mushrooms, 165
Marination, fish for, 23

Mayonnaise
  Easy Blender, 171
  Garlic, 171
    Grilled Mackerel with, 73
    Walnut Garlic, 171
  Scrod Baked with, and Crumbs, 86
Microwave cooking, 40
Mint, Salmon Baked with, 59
Monkfish, 23, 75–76
  Baked with Herbs and Mustard, 76
  general characteristics of, 29–30
  in Inaugural Fish Chowder, 158
  Salad, with Beans and Peppers, 75–76
  in Seafood Salad, 163–64
Monterey Jack cheese
  in Crabmeat with Tomatoes, 133
  in Legal's Lobster Meat Casserole,
    136
  Sole Stuffed with Spinach and, 88–89
Mousse, Scallop, Salmon Fillets Stuffed
    with, 78–79
Mushrooms
  Casserole
    with Haddock, 146
    with Scallops, 145–46
    with Shrimp, 146
  Marinated, 165
  in Monkfish Baked with Herbs and
    Mustard, 76
  Sauce, Wolffish in, 101–2
  in Savory Scrod, 85
  Scallops and, in Stew, 147
  Scrod Stuffed with Shrimp and, 83–84
  Shad Roe with Bacon, Tomatoes and,
    87
  in Sole Stuffed with Crabmeat, 90–91
  in Swordfish Kabobs, 94
  in Swordfish with Summer Vegetables,
    93
Mussels, 106, 138–41
  general characteristics of, 114–16
  au Gratin, 139–40
  in Seafood Salad, 163–64
  Spicy, with Pasta, 140–41
  with Spinach, 144
  Steamed, 138–39
  Swordfish with Tomatoes and, 95
Mustard
  Monkfish Baked with Herbs and, 76
  Sauce, Bluefish with, 61–62

Ocean catfish. See Wolffish

Olive Butter
  Baked Flounder with Ham and, 68
  Broiled Flounder with, 67
Omega-3 fatty acids, 12, 25, 29, 31
Onions
  Mackerel with, and Red Peppers, 74
  Scallops and, in Stew, 146–47
  Onion Strings, 166–67
Orange Sauce, Grilled Swordfish with,
    96–97
Oven steaming, 49–50
Overcooking, 40
  of mussels, 116
  of scallops, 120
  of shrimp, 122
  of squid, 123–25
  See also Cooking time for fish
Overfishing, 13, 27
Oysters, 13, 105, 106, 142–44
  cooking time for, 40
  Fried, 45
  general characteristics of, 117
  on half shell, 119
  shucking, 117–19
  Stew, 142
    with Vegetables, 142
  Stuffed, 142–44
  Swordfish with, 96

Parmesan Cheese, Scrod Baked with,
    and Crumbs, 86
Parmigiana fish, 100–1
  Fresh Tomato Sauce for, 168
Parsley-Garlic Butter, Steamed Clams
    with, 130–31
Pasta
  with Crabmeat Sauce, 134
  Lobster Sauce for, 137
  Scallops with, 134
  Seafood and, Salad, 159–60
  Spicy Clams with, 141
  Spicy Mussels with, 140–41
  in Squid Stuffed with Scallops and
    Red Pepper, 150–51
  Tomato Crabmeat Sauce for, 137
  Two-toned Fettucine with Seafood,
    160–61
Pâté, Smoked Bluefish, 60–61
PCBs, 13, 25
Peaches, Shrimp with Peppers and, 149–
    50

Peppers
  Green
    in Savory Scrod, 84–85
  Italian frying
    Pollock with, and Corn and
      Zucchini, 77
    in Swordfish with Summer
      Vegetables, 93
  Red
    -Garlic Sauce, Fried Squid with,
      152–53
    Mackerel with, and Onions, 74
    Pollock with, and Corn and
      Zucchini, 77
    Shrimp with Peaches and, 149–50
    Squid Stuffed with Scallops and,
      150–51
    Swordfish with Sauce of, and
      Coriander, 80
    Red or Yellow, in Monkfish, Bean, and
      Pepper Salad, 75–76
    Shrimp Sautéed with Coriander and,
      148–49
Poached Salmon, 47–48
Poaching, 46–48
Pollock
  with Corn, Zucchini, and Peppers, 77
  Fish Cakes, 164–65
  in a Fresh Tomato Sauce, 69–70
  Fried, 44–45
  general characteristics of, 30
  as imitation crabmeat, 110
Pollution, 13
  of shellfish, 105–6, 107
Protein in fish, 12

Quahogs, 107

Rainbow trout, 12
Red roe, 114
Refrigeration of fish, 19
Rigor, 17–18

Saffron, in Two-toned Fettucine with
  Seafood, 160–61
Salads
  Crabmeat, 136
  Lobster, 135–36
  Monkfish, with Beans and Peppers,
    75–76
  Seafood, 163–64
  Seafood and Pasta, 159–60

    Marinated Mushrooms for, 165
Squid, 153
  Tuna, Niçoise, 72
  Warm Shellfish, 162–63
Salmon, 12, 24, 78–82
  Baked, with Mint or Dill, 59
  Broiled Coho, with a Chive Butter
    Sauce, 81–82
  Cakes, with Dill, 165
  Chilled, in Soup, with Cucumbers, 79
  cooking time for, 40
  Fillets, Stuffed with Scallop Mousse,
    78–79
  Flounder or Sole Stuffed with, 67
  general characteristics of, 30–31
  Poached, 47–48
  Stuffed Coho, 82
  with a Sweet and Sour Coriander
    Sauce, 80
Salsa, Broiled Swordfish with, 97–98
Salt, 57
Sardines, 12–13
Sauces
  Chive Butter, Broiled Coho Salmon
    with, 81–82
  Cocktail, 167
  Coriander
    and Red Pepper, Swordfish with, 80
    Sweet and Sour, Salmon with, 80
  Crabmeat, Pasta with, 134
  Fresh Tomato, 168
  Guacamole, 64–65
  Lemon-Caper, Fresh Tuna in, 99
  Lobster, for Pasta, 137
  Mushroom, Wolffish in, 101–2
  Mustard, 61–62
  Orange, Grilled Swordfish with, 96–97
  Red Pepper Garlic, Fried Squid with,
    152–53
  Tarragon Cream, Scrod in, 85–86
  Tartar, 169–70
  Tomato, Fresh, Haddock in, 69–70
  Tomato Crabmeat, for Pasta, 137
  Watercress, Halibut with, 71
Sautéed Flounder, 48–49
Sautéed Shad Roe with Lemon and
  Chives, 87–88
Sautéed Shrimp with Coriander and
  Peppers, 148–49
Sautéed Soft-Shell Crabs, 131
Sautéed Sole, 48–49
Sautéing, 23, 48–49

Scallop and Mushroom Stew, 147
Scallop and Onion Stew, 146–47
Scallops, 105, 106, 144–47
    with Basil and Cream, 144–45
    bay (Cape), 120
    Broiled, with Garlic and Lemon, 148
    general characteristics of, 119–20
    Mousse, Salmon Fillets Stuffed with,
        78–79
    Squid Stuffed with, and Red Pepper,
        150–51
Scrod, 26, 32, 83–86
    Baked, 42
        with Cheese and Crumbs, 86
        with Herb Cheese and Crumbs, 86
        with Mayonnaise and Crumbs, 86
        with Tahini and Crumbs, 86
    with Citrus Juices, 63
    in a Fresh Tomato Sauce, 69–70
    Savory, 84–85
    Stuffed with Shrimp and Mushrooms,
        83–84
    in Tarragon Cream Sauce, 85–86
Seafood and Pasta Salad, 159–60
    Marinated Mushrooms for, 165
Seafood Salad, 163–64
Shad, 32
Shad roe, 87–88
    with Bacon, 87
        and Mushrooms and Tomatoes, 87
    general characteristics of, 32–33
    Sautéed, with Lemon and Chives, 87–
        88
Shellfish, 20, 103–53
Shrimp, 106, 147–50
    Broiled, with Garlic, 147–48
        and Tarragon, 148
    Casserole, with Mushrooms, 146
    cocktail, 123
        Sauce for, 167
    Fried, 45
        with Guacamole Sauce, 65
    general characteristics of, 121–23
    in Lobster Milanese, 138
    Maine, 105, 121–22
    with Peaches and Peppers, 149–50
    Sautéed with Coriander and Peppers,
        148–49
    Scrod Stuffed with, and Mushrooms,
        83–84
    Sole Stuffed with, 92
Smoked Bluefish Pâté, 60–61

Sole, 27, 40, 88–92
    Breaded, with Herbs, 90
    with Brown Butter, 49
    Easy Baked, 89
    general characteristics of, 33–34
    with Herbs and Butter, 49
    iodine aftertaste from, 122
    Sautéed, 48
    Stuffed
        with Crabmeat, 90–91
        with Salmon, 67
        with Shrimp, 92
        with Smoked Salmon, 67
        with Spinach and Cheese, 88–89
Soups
    Chilled Salmon and Cucumber, 79
    Clam Chowder, 129–30
    Cod, 63–64
    Inaugural Fish Chowder, 158
Spicy Fried Cusk with Guacamole Sauce,
    64–65
Spinach
    Mussels with, 144
    Sole Stuffed with, and Cheese, 88–89
    in Stuffed Oysters, 142–44
Spinazzola, Anthony, 5
Squid, 106, 150–53
    cleaning, 124–25
    Fried, with Red Pepper Garlic Sauce,
        152–53
    general characteristics of, 123
    Salad, 153
    in Seafood and Pasta Salad, 159–60
    Stuffed with Scallops and Red Pepper,
        150–51
Steamed Cod with Vegetables, 49–50
Steaming, 49–50
    of clams, 107
        with Garlic-Parsley Butter, 130–31
    Mussels, 138–39
Stews, 23
    Oyster, 142
        with Vegetables, 142
    Scallop and Mushroom, 147
    Scallop and Onion, 146–47
    See also Soups
Stock, Fish, 167–68
Stuffed Coho Salmon, 82
Stuffed Oysters, 142–44
Supermarkets, 18
Sweet and Sour Coriander Sauce,
    Salmon in, 80

Swordfish, 23, 93–98
  Broiled, with Salsa, 97–98
  with Coriander and Red Pepper
    Sauce, 80
  general characteristics of, 34
  Grilled, with Orange Sauce, 96–97
  Kabobs, 94–95
  meatlike texture of, 24
  with Oysters, 96
  with Summer Vegetables, 93
  with Tomatoes and Mussels, 95

Tahini, Scrod Baked with, and Crumbs,
    86
Tarragon
  Broiled Shrimp with Garlic and, 148
  Cream Sauce, Scrod in, 85–86
Tartar Sauce, 169–70
Tenderness
  of lobsters, 111–12
  and size of fish, 24
Tomalley, 114
Tomatoes
  in Broiled Swordfish with Salsa, 97–98
  Crabmeat with, 133
  Fresh Sauce, 168
  in Lobster Sauce for Pasta, 137
  in Pasta with Crabmeat Sauce, 134
  Sauce, Fresh, Haddock in, 69–70
  in Savory Scrod, 84–85
  in Seafood and Pasta Salad, 159–60
  Shad Roe with Bacon, Mushrooms
    and, 87
  in Swordfish Kabobs, 94
  Swordfish with, and Mussels, 95
  in Swordfish with Summer Vegetables,
    93
  in Tomato Crabmeat Sauce for Pasta,
    137

Tomato sauce, in fish parmigiana, 100–1
Tuna, 24, 98–99
  bluefin, 12
  Broiled, with Salsa, 98
  Fresh, in a Lemon-Caper Sauce, 99
  general characteristics of, 35
  Grilled, with Cucumber Garnish, 98
  with Lime Juice, 99
  Salad, Niçoise, 72
Two-toned Fettucine with Seafood, 160–
    61

Vegetables
  Flounder Stuffed with, 66–67
  Oyster Stew with, 142
  Steamed Cod with, 49–50
  Summer, Swordfish with, 93
  See also specific vegetables
Vinaigrette, 57

Walnut Garlic Mayonnaise, 171
Warm Shellfish Salad, 162–63
Watercress Sauce, Halibut with, 71
WGBH-T.V., 6–7
Wolffish, 100–2
  general characteristics of, 35
  in Mushroom Sauce, 101–2
  Parmigiana, 100–1

Yogurt, in Chilled Salmon and
    Cucumber Soup, 79

Zinc, 13, 117
Zucchini
  Pollock with, and Corn and Peppers,
    77
  in Savory Scrod, 85